Celebrating Europe

The **Institute of Southeast Asian Studies (ISEAS)** was established as an autonomous organization in 1968. It is a regional centre dedicated to the study of socio-political, security and economic trends and developments in Southeast Asia and its wider geostrategic and economic environment. The Institute's research programmes are the Regional Economic Studies (RES, including ASEAN and APEC), Regional Strategic and Political Studies (RSPS), and Regional Social and Cultural Studies (RSCS).

ISEAS Publishing, an established academic press, has issued more than 2,000 books and journals. It is the largest scholarly publisher of research about Southeast Asia from within the region. ISEAS Publishing works with many other academic and trade publishers and distributors to disseminate important research and analyses from and about Southeast Asia to the rest of the world.

Celebrating Europe
An Asian Journey

ASAD-UL IQBAL LATIF

ISEAS

INSTITUTE OF SOUTHEAST ASIAN STUDIES
Singapore

First published in Singapore in 2012 by ISEAS Publishing
Institute of Southeast Asian Studies
30 Heng Mui Keng Terrace
Pasir Panjang
Singapore 119614

E-mail: publish@iseas.edu.sg
Website: <http://bookshop.iseas.edu.sg>

The responsibility for facts and opinions in this publication rests exclusively with the author and his interpretations do not necessarily reflect the views or the policy of the publisher or its supporters.

ISEAS Library Cataloguing-in-Publication Data

Asad-ul Iqbal Latif.
   Celebrating Europe : an Asian Journey.
   1. Europe—Civilization.
   I. Title.
CB203 L35   2012

ISBN 978-981-4311-50-2 (soft cover)
ISBN 978-981-4311-51-9 (E-book PDF)

Typeset by Superskill Graphics Pte Ltd
Printed in Singapore by Mainland Press Pte Ltd

For
Calcutta Boys' School,
Presidency College, Calcutta
and
Cambridge University

all as old
as
youth itself

Contents

Foreword

Although there is a tendency among some analysts to dismiss Europe as a "has-been", the world in which we live is still shaped by ideas emanating from Europe. This is why it is important for us to augment our knowledge of Europe's contribution to civilization. This effort will enable us to borrow and use facets of the European experience and transform them into building blocks around the world. Perhaps even the Europeans could take heart and gain courage by looking at their own past!

The European Union is today buffeted by a financial storm never seen in its history. However, Europe's past tells Europeans that, even though they are struggling to overcome a calamitous economic situation, there is no reason for despair. The "old continent" has overcome worse challenges and has come out stronger and more mature. Indeed, it has been purified by threats that were directed at the plinth of what Europe stands for. Well-wishers of Europe hope that its union will endure and prove to be a permanent contribution to world peace.

Seen from the outside, Europe is vast collection of nation-states, regions, some reminiscences from the past, and, of course, the European Union, which encompasses 27 countries. However, Europe is more than the European Union. European ideals, cultivated over centuries, have benefited from diversity, the continent's great strength.

The European Union has tried to define what it stands for. I quote from its proposed Constitution: "The Union is founded on the values of respect for human dignity, freedom, democracy, equality, the rule of law and respect for human rights, including the rights of persons belonging to minorities. These values are common to the Member States in a society in which pluralism, non-discrimination, tolerance, justice, solidarity and equality between women and men prevail."

These principles are a valuable contribution to the making of a better world. Europe today offers a mixture of political freedom, respect for human rights, and a genuine wish to find solutions to global problems such as global warming and poverty. These are values that transcend time and space, although their application outside Europe depends on time and place.

It is that Europe which Asad-ul Iqbal Latif celebrates in this book. He has been a prolific writer since he joined ISEAS in 2005. His books have focused on several international and historical issues: Singapore's position between China and India; the possible formation of a triangle linking Singapore to India and the United States; and India's role in the making of Singapore. He has written on domestic issues as well in his biography of first-generation Singapore leader Lim Kim San and his book on Singapore's Community Engagement Programme.

In this study, Asad draws on his intellectual encounters with Europe as a student, a traveller and a Europhile. He combines his personal experiences with a keen cultural insight into the idea of Europe and what makes it worthy of celebration.

He does not gloss over terrible episodes in Europe's interaction with other countries and even its own people.

Colonialism and the Holocaust are discussed vividly in the book. However, on balance, the European project remains an integral contribution to the evolution of universal humanism.

It is that European project which Asad celebrates movingly in this bittersweet book — a little bitter but far more sweet.

K. Kesavapany
Director
Institute of Southeast Asian Studies

Acknowledgements

The sections in this book on my visit to France are drawn from an article, "French heaven on earth", that was originally published in *The Sunday Times* on 8 August 2004. *Source: The Sunday Times © Singapore Press Holdings Limited. Reprinted with permission.*

Introduction: Europe

The world is in large part a European invention. Europe has
created, named, and shaped every historical era, from the
classical world and the Middle Ages, to the Renaissance,
the Reformation, and their culmination in the modern age
of the nation-state, and now to the postmodern lease of life
promised by the supranationalism of the European Union.[1]
It is instructive that Europeans — and only Europeans
— have succeeded in travelling beyond the nation-state into
a quasi-federal union.[2] It took two world wars — Europe's
two great "civil wars"[3] — to set that process of integration
in motion through the transnational control of coal and
steel, two commodities that are crucial to the conduct of
modern warfare. Certainly, the collective idea of Europe
as an inherited political and cultural domain is marked
by great contention and contest, but this disagreement is
natural because, like all identities, the identity of Europe
is constructed around "shifting discursive practices" that
emerge from a rich register of political, cultural, and
economic languages.[4]

The chapters that follow constitute a modest attempt to
relate an Asian's encounters with Europe. My understanding
of Europe was mediated by my family's experience of
the contradictory British impulses of colonialism and
liberalism; that understanding was nuanced later by

my student life at Cambridge, to which I went, following in my father's footsteps. Two chapters in the book are about Britain. Europe's colonial depredations were echoed in the horrors of the Holocaust, which form the subject of an early chapter. The chapter, "Gentiles", is a defence of the intellectual basis of European secularism in the face of the international assault mounted by confessional societies and their states. It examines how secularism was crucial to the very evolution of Europe as a civilization; how the secular impulse is related to the struggle between Hebraism and Hellenism for the European imagination; how that struggle has evolved into the ironic sense of life (compared with the tragic sense of life); and what some implications of the ironic life might be for Europe's role as a sanctuary for dissidence and heresy today. In this context, the Swiss vote in favour of banning the construction of mosque minarets grates on the secular sensibility, as it should. However, why are the reflexes of societies such as those of the Swiss, the Dutch, and the French, societies that are disposed liberally towards both belief and disbelief, hardening against members of an immigrant religion? In posing this question, a commentator argues that the point is not to wonder how liberal societies could behave in this way, but to understand that they behave in this way precisely because they are liberal.[5] That is a disturbing thought, but one that cannot be dismissed.

   The agency of secularism cannot be detached from that of liberty as a governing principle in the life of nations. The recognition inherent in secularism — that the state is not mandated to impose religious beliefs on its citizens even if most of them treat those beliefs as absolute truths — finds its political expression in the essence of liberty, which is that nothing is inevitable, let alone permanent, in history — because, just as men have made their history, they are free to change it. Hence there is no perfect or final form of government or society. Instead, history is the graveyard of absolutes. The chapter on *The Leopard* analyses the mood of political mortality present in a great Italian historical novel based on the confrontation between feudal nobility in decay and the bourgeoisie that seeks to replace it. The chapters on the Fall of the Berlin Wall and the Fall of the Soviet Union derive fundamentally from questions about the nature of history. The first fall released around the world an exhilarating sense of peoples' liberation from a totalitarian system. That liberation was followed soon, however, by a palpable sense of loss over the second fall, with which the greatest attempt in history to liberate man from exploitation by man disappeared.

That story has not ended. When the Soviet Union disappeared, so did the Soviet empire, in an implosion that freed Marxism-Leninism to resume its theoretical journey towards being an international rendezvous again. Thus, in a review of Michael Hardt's and Antonio Negri's *Empire*, Gopal Balakrishnan writes of "a world overflowing with insurgent energies" that has embarked on "a Long March against the new scheme of things".[6] Hardt and Negri find ancient genealogies at work in this scheme of things: American nuclear superiority embodies the monarchical reality; the economic wealth of the Group of Seven industrialized states and transnational corporations represents the aristocratic element; and the Internet brings tidings of the democratic principle. Today's world is the allegorical inheritor of the later Roman Empire, where Christians witnessed the "inexorable hollowing out of the terrestrial order of things and the beginnings of a new, rejuvenating era of barbarian migrations".[7] In that unfolding context, my Bengali Greeks are two young lovers in Calcutta whose politics hark back to a tradition that is much older than the Roman Empire, a tradition produced by the Athenian quest for an erotic *polis* where the love of two mortals for each other would form the pathway for love between citizens and the state.

The last chapter is an impressionistic view of the prospects of postmodern Europe. The idea of Europe is shaped by the cafés that dot its geography, George Steiner remarks elliptically, by way of capturing the spirit of a continent mapped by Pessoa's favourite Lisbon cafeteria, and Kierkgaard's Copenhagen cafés. Europe will exist so long as its cafés do.[8] Indeed, these veritable "clubs of the mind" have set the scene for some of the founding moments of contemporary Europe, moments such as Casanova's erotic trysts in the Venetian Florian, Sartre's rendezvous with existentialism at the lucky Café Flore, or Byron's high tea at Rome's Antico Caffè Greco, which drew also Schopenhauer, Wagner, Henry James, and Leopardi.[9] Europe owes a great deal to the café.

This, too, is a café kind of book. It germinated in the *adda*, that quintessentially Bengali art of conversation between consenting adults which takes place at coffee houses, street corners and street-corner tea houses. The book came of age in late-night trysts with books at home, insomniacs like me. It took shape in the tea houses and coffee shops of Calcutta and Cambridge and Singapore, and in cafés that I have visited only in the Europes of my mind.

What draws me to Europe is not just the quality of its intellectual life: That quality is present elsewhere as well. It is that the European intellectual displays a normative disquiet, born of a deep and stubborn refusal to be happy at others' expense, that keeps the Old Continent at the forefront of the newest existential agendas. Rob Riemen writes gracefully about the permanence of this European legacy in his *Nobility of Spirit: A Forgotten Ideal*, a book that should become a celebrated text of what Europe can stand for if it reaches up for its legacy.[10] Needless to say, there also are European realities that fall far short of the ideals. That is true particularly of culture. Walter Benjamin noted that the cultural treasures which man surveys share, without exception, a horrible origin. "There is no document of civilization which is not at the same time a document of barbarism."[11] It took twentieth-century Europe's most civilized and filial son to say that. The best indictments of Europe continue to be European. The secular parables of Roland Barthes' *Mythologies*[12] parody the almost shamanistic bewitchment and bewilderment of the European amidst the signs, signals, symbols, gestures, and messages through which society legitimates and sustains its myths and beliefs by obscuring its realities to itself.[13] However, there would have been no point to his delightfully abrasive mockery without a serious belief in a humane European universe that is recoverable from the excesses of universalized European history. The Indian poet laureate Rabindranath Tagore put this succinctly when, in lectures delivered during World War I that warned against

the East copying the fratricidal nationalism of colonial
Europe, he said nevertheless:

> There is one safety for us upon which we hope we may
> count, and that is that we can claim Europe herself as our
> ally in our resistance to her temptations and to her violent
> encroachments; for she has ever carried her own standard of
> perfection, by which we can measure her falls and gauge her
> degrees of failure, by which we can call her before her own
> tribunal and put her to shame — the shame which is the sign
> of the true pride of nobleness.[14]

It is interesting that for both Tagore and Rieman, it is
nobility/nobleness that is the characteristic quality of
Europe. That nobility is best revealed under the most intense
questioning.

Unfortunately, the radical scepticism without which
Europe would be nothing is being hollowed out by a kind
of comfortable, boutique nihilism because of which, one
day, Europe will be nothing. My humble work is an attempt
to plead otherwise, to suggest that there is much in the
European experience that is of enduring value to Europeans
and others alike, and that the undermining of Europe does
not contribute to a healthy universalism.

This book is a statement of an Asian's hope for, and
stake in, a humane universe informed by the best in European
civilization.

Notes

1. Parag Khanna, "A Postmodern Middle Ages", *Spiegel* Online,
    23 July 2009, <http://www.spiegel.de/international/europe/
    0,1518,druck-637830,00.html>.

2. Craig Parsons, *A Certain Idea of Europe* (Ithaca: Cornell University Press, 2006).

3. Salvador de Madariaga, *Portrait of Europe* (New York: Roy Publishers, 1955), p. 23.

4. Anthony Pagden (ed.), *The Idea of Europe: From Antiquity to the European Union* (Cambridge: Cambridge University Press, 2002), p. 1.

5. Rod Liddle, "It's not just the Swiss — all Europe is ready to revolt", *The Spectator*, 2 December 2009, <http://www.spectator.co.uk/spectator/5592733/its-not-just-the-swiss-all-europe-is-ready-to-revolt.thtml>.

6. Gopal Balakrishnan, "Virgilian Visions", *New Left Review* 5, September/October 2000, p. 143; p. 142.

7. Ibid., p. 144.

8. George Steiner, *The Idea of Europe* (Amsterdam: Nexus Institute, 2005).

9. Joana Bonet, "Starbucks Democracy", *La Vanguardia*, 10 June 2009, <http://www.presseurop.eu/en/content/article/24111-starbucks-democracy>.

10. Rob Riemen, *Nobility of Spirit: A Forgotten Ideal*, Foreword by George Steiner (New Haven: Yale University Press, 2009).

11. Walter Benjamin, *Illuminations*, translated by Harry Zohn (New York: Schocken Books, 2007), p. 256.

12. Roland Barthes, *Mythologies*, selected and translated from French by Annette Lavers (London: Paladin Books, 1973). Roland Barthes, *The Eiffel Tower and Other Mythologies*, translated by Richard Howard (Berkeley: University of California Press, 1977), is equally invigorating.

13. Dennis Potter, *The Times*, cited in ibid.

14. Rabindranath Tagore, *Nationalism*, with an introduction by Ramachandra Guha (New Delhi: Penguin Books India, 2009), p. 30.

1
Europe Abroad

The East is a career
— Benjamin Disraeli

Sheikh Abdullah was a prosperous landowner and trader in the Hooghly district of undivided Bengal. He was a devout Muslim. In the course of his business pursuits during the British Raj, he once had to meet an Englishman. What would happen if he had to shake the pork-eater's hand, he wondered darkly. He asked his wife, a kindly matriarch who made certain that a portion of her husband's income found its way to the poor in their village. Charity needed an income, she reasoned. So she advised him to shake the dreaded hand, strike a deal, come back home, wash himself seven times with soil, pray, and hope to be absolved. So he did.

Mohamed Abdul Latif, one of their eight children, was born in 1921. He studied at Hare School in Calcutta. Set up in 1818 by two reformers — the Scottish David Hare and the Bengali Raja Ram Mohun Roy — the school made available in the vernacular all that Western education offered in English during the Raj.

Then came London. Arriving there in 1938, he was struck by the freedom of speech the British enjoyed. He decided to exercise his own freedom of speech at the London School of Economics, where he had enrolled.

One of his teachers was Professor Harold Laski. Latif could not bear Professor Laski's Fabian Socialism because, by urging the rich to coexist conscientiously with the poor, it forced the poor to coexist unconscientiously with the rich. Fabian fables were exactly what capital needed to keep real socialism at bay, he thought. Yet Professor Laski was being feted by the world. One day, Latif let go in the students' room: "Laski is a swine."

The professor heard about the abuse. Accustomed to the adulation of his students, he was shocked. The teacher in him called out, no doubt, for disciplinary action, but the man of ideas in him sought an explanation for the outburst. He asked Latif to see him. When he did, Laski asked him whether he would apologize for his appalling conduct. Latif apologized for his conduct, but not for his views. He said that he considered Professor Laski and people like him a menace to socialism. Had not the Nazis copied John Maynard Keynes' economic programme? How could a man be a socialist of any kind if he appealed to fascists? As for Professor Laski's fabled Fabianism, all that it would do for independent India would be to sanctify the transfer of power from a colonial ruling class to a local one. The professor would give his blessings to the faked death of the British Raj, and a reborn Indian Raj would invoke his name gratefully in return. How fetching, this mutual admiration! Was this to be his legacy to socialism from the historic ramparts of the LSE?

The professor took his precocious critic seriously, and began to question Latif on whether his Manichean vision of socialism was any more applicable to India's economic and political stage of development than was the compromise he berated. A conversation ensued. Even months later, neither side conceded defeat.

A letter of reference from a singular man, the magnanimous Laski, helped Latif's application to Cambridge, to which he went up in 1943 to read Law and Economics at Jesus College. Life in wartime Cambridge was an education in itself. He made friends with Ram Cohen, whose sparkling mind and warm companionship protected him from the very weather. Cohen died while saving his girlfriend during a German bombing raid.

At one point, Latif found himself lodging in the home of the Handleys — good, honest, and strong people who represented the best of working-class England. They never hurried him for the rent when his family's remittances from India were delayed; instead, they fed him some of the bread, butter, and eggs from their own wartime rations. The Handleys had a daughter, Nora, but no son, and Handley called Latif "my boy". The family was above race. When a neighbour ran to the missus one day, saying "I saw Nora walking hand in hand with a black man" – the lady replied: "I know, my dear. I asked them to."

Latif passed his examinations and was called to the Bar from Lincoln's Inn. His parents wanted him to take the Indian Civil Service examinations, but he had other plans. He left Cambridge with his degree and the old quip that people at Oxford behave as if they own the world, while people at Cambridge behave as if they do not care who owns the world. He certainly did not care. No "as if" there.

Barrister Latif's return to India in 1946 was not a propitious one. Most of his books, which he had kept in a brother's shop in Calcutta, were destroyed in the terrible communal riots of that year. However, although India won freedom a year later amidst a bloodbath, it was freedom nevertheless, and I was born a free human in 1957 in Calcutta.

Europe's World

Europe's mythical origins lie in Zeus' abduction of the Asian princess Europa. The cultural impulses of imperialism were ancient. "Asia suffers, yet in its suffering it threatens Europe: the eternal, bristling frontier endures between East and West, almost unchanged since classical antiquity", Edward Said writes movingly in *Orientalism.*[1] Asia sits, brooding, on the ontological threshold; Europe watches, unmoved. Yet, Asia played a crucial role in the making of Europe. A global political economy, emerging in the sixteenth century, brought European monarchies into increasingly sustained relations with one another, deepening relations between the stronger and weaker states in the emerging European (and, later, international) state system, and coinciding with a division of labour between the increasingly core and peripheral areas of the world system.[2] Europe looked outward in its voyages of discovery, which came to be buoyed by the expansive self-confidence of capitalism. From the late 1840s to the mid-1870s, these developments had coalesced into an era in which the mission was to unify the world. Eric Hobsbawm writes elegantly of how industrial capitalism became a world economy and how the globe metamorphosed "from

a geographical entity into a constant operational reality".[3]
There came into existence men who "thought in continents
and oceans. For them the world was then a single unit, bound
together with rails of iron and steam engines, because the
horizons of business were like their dreams world-wide".[4]
History from then became world history.[5] Colonialism
sought out alien spaces that it could domesticate through
trade, religion, education, control, conquest, and the ultimate
presence, settlement. Colonies became markers of domestic
power; their subordination represented the metropole's
reach into the world, and its determination to reorder it as
an extensive unity.

The economic prosperity and technological advance
associated with capitalism provided the material impetus
for European expansion. In being the agent of this impetus,
the Industrial Revolution exported abroad what it had
inaugurated at home: an era of social dislocation and
suffering, of human degradation and despair. European
imperialism devastated the economic, social, and religious
landscape of much of the non-Western world. If the
Enlightenment stood for a universal rationality, it stood
also for a universal civilization based on the salvation
of non-Christian souls and the capture of non-European
lands. The genocidal clearing of ancestral American spaces,
inhabited by the tribes of the "discovered" New World,
had made room once for the dislodged tribes of Europe's
Old World. The method was replicated in the conveniently
demarcated *terra nullius* — the land belonging to no one
— of Australia, which provided the terrain for another wave
of settler colonialism. In between these extremes of the New
World and the Antipodes, European merchants, mercenaries,

and missionaries descended on the mindscapes of Asia and Africa, visiting on the chosen objects of *la mission civilisatrice* the benedictions of war, famine, destitution, and decrepitude. Europe transformed itself and the West into a universal idea, not through the arcadian spread of its best values — scepticism, freedom, and secularism — but on the back of its worst vices: mercantilism, racism, and religious fanaticism.

Anti-colonial nationalism did try to reverse the colonial logic. Like anti-imperialism generally, anti-colonialism sought to roll back alien political frontiers in order to free a single, shared, global space of the suffocating presence of domination. It saw its mission as the ejection of a trespasser, a recovery and purification of lost and polluted native space. This mission could assume a physical form, as when political space was reclaimed by overcoming distance, notably in Mao Zedong's Long March, but also in Mahatma Gandhi's Dandi March. The Ho Chi Minh Trail was the lifeline of a revolutionary effort that turned Vietnam, one country situated at a particular conjuncture, into a shorthand description of an entire historical process.

However, the Third World nation generally remained a state-sponsored space and that, too, one inherited from colonial administrative structures and strictures. Third World nationalism remained a derivative discourse. Calls for the "de-imperialization of the state" in Africa were ignored or found themselves diverted harmlessly into the *negritude* movement, a form of "pastoral idyllism" that romanticized the African past. Wole Soyinka ridiculed *negritude* as *tigritude* when he wrote: "I don't think a tiger has to go around proclaiming his tigritude."[6] But it did, and as it did so, the Orient remained a partial creation of the Occident, continuing to seek itself in its very partiality through its obsession with the West. Through the incestuous nexus of trade, religion, control, conquest, and education, Europe almost unmade Asia.

Thus, Claude Lévi-Strauss writes in *Tristes Tropiques* of a visit to Bengal, a region that bears contemporary witness to history's "most tragic phases of development": "the shortages and epidemics of medieval times, frenzied exploitation as in the early years of the industrial revolution, and the unemployment and speculation of modern capitalism".[7] On a journey to the Chittagong Hills, in the then-Pakistani province of East Bengal, where people ate two humble meals a day, he refused to partake of five sumptuous diurnal repasts. His frugality scandalized his companion, a Buddhist aristocrat educated in an Anglo-Indian school. As Lévi-Strauss explained French eating habits, he sensed the upheaval that he was causing in the chap's mind: "a white man could, after all, be just a man".[8] The brown man's refusal to understand equality developed almost sexual undertones during a trip that Lévi-Strauss made to the regional capital, Dacca. He found himself the guest of a young teacher who was presiding over his wife's emancipation from *purdah*. The husband pelted her with sarcastic remarks, the tactlessness of which embarrassed Lévi-Strauss as much as it did her. There was more. "Since I was an anthropologist, he made her bring out her personal underwear from a modest little chest-of-drawers, so that I could note the different items," the father of structural anthropology exclaims in disbelief. "With a little encouragement he would have made her undress in front of me, so anxious was he to prove his esteem for Western ways, of which he knew nothing."[9]

But why was Lévi-Strauss so disturbed by the ignorant teacher or the obsequious aristocrat? They were unable to bear the burden of equality because they were products of a European discourse that was inherently unequal. The whole point of what Edward Said identifies as Orientalism — the West's imperial production of knowledge about the East — was to incorporate the East into the Western imagination, absorb it into Western discourse, and contain it as a reality in itself and for itself.[10] The East became itself when it saw itself through the eyes of the West. In the era of colonialism, knowledge and power conspired imperiously with each other as never before, or since, to produce the East as a lucky subject whose liberation from its rotting past lay in its ability to mimic the life of the West. Naturally, then, the mutant inventions of the West sought their sense of reality in the fictions of the West. It was by flaunting their ascribed and internalized inferiority that they gained access to its mercies, myths, and mysteries. In the circumstances, proximity to an actual Western creation — be he a scholar, a sailor, a swindler, or a savant — provoked in the creations of Orientalism rhapsodic delusions of cultural salvation. Some fell to feeding their godlike guests the imagined feasts of Greece and Rome; others produced their wives' underwear for inspection as totems of sexual liberation. It was the West that had produced these caricatures.

The Mace

However, the West also produced antidotes for its own caricatures. Take me, for example. I inherited England vicariously from my father, as a form of liberation from the British empire. I associated England with liberty because my father had travelled to that country in search of India's freedom. It was in places such as LSE and Cambridge, proof of England's claims to being the home of liberty, that some of the sharpest indictments of England's war on Indian liberty were possible.

It was liberty that had produced the equality that allowed a student to disagree passionately with his teacher — and be rewarded for it. A Bengali Muslim could be equal to a British Jew in the republic of ideas although Britain was a monarchy that squatted on India. What Professor Laski had taught his prodigal student was the political virtue of agreeing to disagree. The student had dismissed this teaching as a bourgeois compromise, but he understood later that democracy requires just this quality of tolerance. Without the theoretical equality of opinions — till one side resorts to violence or is proved irremediably wrong — parliamentary democracy, for example, is impossible. What England offered was a formal parliamentary model which showed that it was possible to disagree over ends while agreeing on means.

I owe my hands-on experience of parliamentary democracy to my father, who ran successfully in the 1967 and 1969 elections to the West Bengal Legislative Assembly. As a present for my approaching twelfth birthday, he took me along to watch an Assembly sitting in July 1969. The Maoist Naxalite movement was in full swing, and yet another policeman had been killed. A group of protesting policemen brought the body of the slain man to the Assembly, demanding firm action from the government. Up in the press gallery, where my father had deposited me, I watched in horror as the policemen broke through the door of the

Chamber and began to beat up everyone and everything in sight. Legislators, including the Speaker, ran helter-skelter in a legislature rent asunder by the lawlessness of the law.

In the midst of the commotion, someone caught my terrified eye. This was the humble Bearer of the Mace, who was running *towards* the police. His objective was to rescue the Mace. Having done so, he cradled as if it were his child. The Speaker did not matter, my father did not matter, I did not matter, and even the Bearer himself did not matter. What mattered was the Mace, the symbol of parliamentary authority. Assemblymen would come and go, but the Assembly must go on forever. As the poor Bearer ran back from the marauding police with the Mace firmly in his arms, lo and behold, even they held back from beating him! Such was the power of an inanimate object in the fractious democracy of men.

I ran out of the press gallery, which had emptied by then, and hid in a toilet. I heard the sound of policemen making their way up the stairs. Soon, one of them was on the floor, daring any legislator to come out. Suddenly, as I cowered in the toilet with my hands over my head, a six-foot demon appeared with his baton raised. Seeing me, he brought it down, but stopped, his trained reflexes interposing in the split second between anger and the sight of a child. He ran out. I, too, did, and found my father soon afterwards. He had a cut in his arm, and his *dhuti-panjabi* — the Bengali dress he wore to the Assembly — was crumpled and soiled.

One good thing came out of my experiences that day. I got to meet Clifford Hicks, Principal of Calcutta Boys' School, who, as a representative of the Anglo-Indian community, was a Nominated Member of the Legislative Assembly. This fearsome disciplinarian had introduced a motto when he had taken over as principal in 1953: "Two yards outside the school gates, the jungle begins." Now, in the Assembly, he knew just how prescient he had been. Hicks had managed to survive the day's events without injury. As my father and I met him on the way out, he asked me to describe my experience of the session. My commentary, rather than description, was vivid enough for him to think that I was good at composition. Our meeting helped, I believe, when he decided to admit me to the school later.

I inhabited the press gallery later as an adult, as a reporter for *The Statesman*. I wished that I had been a journalist earlier, to tell the story of a Bengali boy's first encounter with that very European animal called parliamentary democracy.

English as a Father Tongue

Parameshwara Raghava Kurup and Nilima Kurup lived in the same block of flats in Calcutta that my parents did. Kurup, a Malayalee, and his wife (nee Bose), a Bengali, were childless. So when I appeared in the flat on the floor above theirs, I became their child as well. The lady became *jethima* ("aunt" in Bengali), but Kurup, who properly should have become *jathamoshai*, became *jathaba*. There was logic in the nomenclature. *Ma* is "mother" in Bengali, and *ba* was but an abbreviation of *baba*, or "father" in the same language. They became my second set of parents.

I would have imbibed the English ideas of liberty and tolerance in Bengali, my mother-tongue, which I spoke with my parents and *jethima*, but for the presence of *jathaba*, who spoke no Bengali. As I climbed onto his lap and drew his face towards mine, his smile-formed words shaped themselves into a language called English. He gave me a father-tongue.

Fluent in Sanskrit and well versed in the Vedas, Kurup had left his home in Kerala at the age of fifteen after a quarrel with his father. Arriving in England as a young man, he studied at King's College in the University of London, where he joined up with radical, but non-communist student groups that were committed to bidding swift adieu to the British Raj. In Calcutta, Kurup met his wife-to-be. Nilima Bose's father had deserted the family for the life of an ascetic when she had been a child. Her mother had brought her up, along with her elder sister and younger brother, in the home of a relative. The young Nilima possessed a keenly independent streak and rebuffed offers of marriage from pompous and usurious Bengali men looking for a domestic slave. Instead, she looked at India's fight against colonial Britain as the macrocosm of her own struggle for selfhood. Her heroes were freedom-fighters such as Bina Das, who in 1932 had shot at, but had failed to assassinate Governor Stanley Jackson of Bengal; Surya Sen, leader of the Chittagong Armoury Raid of 1930; and Subhas Chandra Bose. Bose, especially, was an iconic figure for her because the mysterious circumstances of his death had led many Bengalis to believe that he was alive and would return to independent India one day. Perhaps *jethima* believed that her own father would reappear one sudden day from the mountains into which he had vanished, in a microcosmic enactment of Bose's grand return to India.

More than anyone else whom I know, she hated British imperialism personally, with intensity akin to what Herbert Marcuse called the biological hatred that lies at the heart of class warfare.

And here lay the irony of ironies. *Jethima* was attracted to *jathaba* because he had read English at King's College; he spoke English with an effortlessly patrician accent; and, most of all, this tall, dark and very handsome man was committed to the building of a new India from the ashes of the imperialism that had taught him English. To her, he represented the best of the British way of life — a suspicion of ideological extremes, respect for the law, loathing for hypocrisy, cant and humbug, an innate sense of fair play, and sympathy for the underdog — without its worst aspects: parochialism, racism, and colonialism. They fell in love and married.

Jathaba drew *jethima* to his encounters with Chaucer, Shakespeare, Marlowe, Webster, Dryden, Pope, Wordsworth, Eliot, and Yeats. As she moved towards her bachelor's degree and her master's degree examinations in English, she read aloud from the texts. I grew up imbibing first the sound and then the sense of *The Canterbury Tales*, *Antony and Cleopatra*, *Doctor Faustus*, *The Duchess of Malfi*, *All for Love*, *The Dunciad*, *The Prelude*, *Murder in the Cathedral*, and *The Second Coming*. As English was the father-tongue I had inherited from *jathaba*, it was wonderfully apposite that *jethima* should introduce me to its literature aurally. Fathers are language; mothers are literature.

Jathaba died in 1971. My marks in school began to go downhill. Changing subject-streams and schools, I joined Calcutta Boys' School in 1973. Under the supervision of

Hicks, William Torrick, who taught us English Language, Kodaikanal, who taught us English Literature, Guha, who taught even me Mathematics, Jyanapriya Ghosh, whose free tuition classes made him a most non-commercial teacher of Commercial Studies, and others, I did well in the Senior Cambridge examinations and was eligible to *apply* to read English Honours at Presidency College, Calcutta. *Jethima* was delighted and threw a party for my school friends. The next step was to take the entrance examination to Presidency College, but I wrote myself off as more than 200 people were clamouring for fifteen places and, going by the claims some made, they were descended from Shakespeare on one side and Tagore on the other. I got in and never saw them again. *Jethima* was ecstatic. The surrogate son of an enemy of British imperialism had got into the finest department for the study of English in free India.

Notes

1. Edward W. Said, *Orientalism: Western Conceptions of the Orient* (Harmondsworth: Penguin, 1985), p. 250.
2. "Patterns of Development of the Modern World System", a research proposal, in *Review* 1, 2 (Fall 1977), p. 113. Classic expositions of this theme remain Immanuel Wallerstein, *The Modern World System: Capitalist Agriculture and the Origins of the European World Economy in the Sixteenth Century* (New York and London: Academic Press, 1997); *The Modern World System II: Mercantilism and the Consolidation of the European World-Economy, 1600–1750* (New York: Academic Press, 1980); *The Modern World System III: The Second Era of Great Expansion of the Capitalist World-Economy, 1730–1840s* (San Diego: Academic Press, 1989); and *The Capitalist World Economy* (Cambridge University Press, Cambridge 1979).

3. Eric Hobsbawm, *The Age of Capital: 1948–1875* (New York: Vintage Books, 1996), p. 47.

4. Ibid., p. 57.

5. Ibid., p. 47.

6. Jan Nederveen Pieterse and Bhikhu Parekh, "Shifting Imaginaries: Decolonization, Internal Decolonization, Postcoloniality", in Jan Nederveen Pieterse and Bhikhu Parekh, eds., *The Decolonization of Imagination: Culture, Knowledge and Power* (London and New Jersey: Zed Books, 1995), p. 8.

7. Claude Lévi-Strauss, *Tristes Tropiques*, translated from the French by John and Doreen Weightman (New York: Penguin Books, 1992), p. 148.

8. Ibid., p. 141.

9. Ibid., p. 129.

10. Said, *Orientalism*, op. cit., p. 250.

2
Gentiles

No poetry after Auschwitz
— Theodor Adorno

To the question "What are you writing?" my answer was:
"A writer, children, is someone who writes against
the passage of time."
— Günter Grass

The Yad Vashem Holocaust History Museum in Jerusalem is purgatory. One goes there to pay for other people's sins, but comes out purified all the same. One emerges a Jew. The photographic exhibits soon overwhelm the senses; one grows immune to the tragic residues of suffering because suffering is depicted on such an epic scale and, therefore, diffused. But it was a single photograph that rescued my mind from numbness. It showed a group of Jews, spanning several generations, who had been photographed just before they were to be transported to a concentration camp. Their faces betrayed none of the emotions that could be expected of humans in such a situation. They did not exhibit even the calmness of resignation. They looked at the camera with a calmness approaching calmness itself. It was as if the occasion could not have been more normal. True, the condemned all wore a plaintive look, but it was the plaintiveness of tourists posing for a group photograph at the end of a holiday cut short by an inexplicable act of nature. The holiday had brought them to a wonderful place that they liked very much and were loathe to leave, but the holiday would have come to an end in any case. So they were going home. They merely wished they could have stayed a little longer.

I could not take it any more and ran out of the museum. It was almost as if I were running towards Europe. *"Men are accomplices to that which leaves them indifferent,"* George Steiner writes. "It is this fact which must, I think, make the Jew wary inside Western culture, which must lead him to re-examine ideals and historical traditions that, certainly in Europe, had enlisted the best of his hopes and genius. The house of civilization proved no shelter."[1] This is what Europe had done to the Jews.

As I came out of the museum, I saw a young visitor — perhaps, like me, a foreigner on his first visit there — sitting on the ground and sobbing uncontrollably. Rachel had wailed for her children: This man was crying for six million children of the Jewish race lost in the Shoah, the calamity of Nazi persecution, expulsion, and destruction that now defined the identity of every Jew eternally. A tear-borne eternity flowed from the eyes of a single man in Yad Vashem. Although it was sunny, his body was racked with sobs as if the harshest winter of European history had entered his bones and was gnawing away at them, from deep within the Jewish marrow that made him human.

It was 1994. I was among a group of Asian journalists whom the Israeli government had invited to discuss the possibilities of Arab-Israeli peace. Politically, it was spring, for the hopes aroused at Oslo were very much in the air, but an evil chill from Auschwitz and Belsen-Bergen, from Buchenwald and Dachau, from Theresienstadt and Treblinka, crept into my soul.

The helplessness captured in the photograph embodied what Hannah Arendt calls, incomparably, "the banality of evil" in her book on Adolf Eichmann's trial in Jerusalem. In a work that helped establish the truth that it is criminal to carry out criminal orders, she describes wherein this banality lay. It lay in the fact that Nazism had made barbarism something normal, as if eugenics were little more than a variety of municipal planning, as if the "Final Solution" were just another policy among the thousands that states adopt habitually. The problem with Eichmann was that so many were like him, "and that the many were neither perverted nor sadistic, that they were, and still are, terribly and terrifyingly normal".[2] Indeed, Eichmann had a conscience, which functioned like one for about four weeks, "whereupon it began to function the other way around".[3]

In less than two years from December 1939, about 50,000 mentally sick Germans were killed with carbon monoxide gas in a grim prelude to the "euthanasia" of Jews. Banality shines best in the euphemisms that adorn it: In both cases, the Nazis described gassing as the humane way of killing people by granting them a mercy death.[4] The banality of evil explains the unremarkable professionalism that Eichmann brought to his job. Like Hitler, Eichmann had Jewish friends; indeed, he tried to save some of them. But when he dutifully sent other Jews to their death, he found it as normal as trying to save his friends. It is normalcy that

Steiner castigates when he writes: "We know that a man can read Goethe or Rilke in the evening, that he can play Bach and Schubert, and go to his day's work in Auschwitz in the morning." What the Nazi evil did was to call into question the very belief in humane literacy, the axiomatic hope held from Plato's time to Matthew Arnold's that "the energies of spirit are transferable to those of conduct".[5] Unless normalcy intervenes. Banality explains the general German complicity in what Günter Grass calls "the German crime".[6] Nazism was evil: The wider German ability to treat it as somewhat natural in the scheme of things made the evil banal.

Indeed, it is the all-enveloping banality of evil that helps explain, not only the abysmal failure of Jewish leadership in those wildest and cruellest of times, but also, to some extent at least, the equanimity with which the Nazis' Jewish collaborators helped round up Jews for deportation and/or extermination — in full knowledge that their own turn would come. Banality explains the ease with which people could contemplate their own approaching deaths with a logical detachment bordering on indifference. Jews laboriously filled in forms on their property (so that it could be seized later) before boarding trains ritually — to leave for their own funeral.[7] Of course, Eichmann did not expect the Jews to "share the general enthusiasm over their destruction", but "he did expect more than compliance, he expected — and received, to a truly extraordinary degree — their cooperation".[8] The degree to which even Jews accepted the standards of the "Final Solution"[9] — the extent to which, in modern parlance, they internalized their situation — was terrifying, except that there was no word for this terror. It was a voiceless pair of lips, a shape resigned to silence. The silence produced a kind of staccato among those allowed to speak. Elements of the cultural elite lamented that Germany had sent Einstein into exile, "without realizing that it was a much greater crime to kill little Hans Cohn from around the corner, even though he was no genius".[10]

Sartre famously called the Jewish problem a Gentile problem.[11] This is true, but it is one of history's most terrible ironies that the concept of a chosen people, "of a nation exalted over others by particular destiny", was born in Israel. Nazism parodied the Judaic claim vengefully. "The theological motif of a people elected at Sinai is echoed in the pretence of the master race and its chiliastic dominion," Steiner writes. "Thus there was in the obsessed relation of Nazi to Jew a minute but fearful grain of logic."[12] Gentiles long had constructed Jews in the hostile image of Otherness: The Nazis took it upon themselves to try and erase this Otherness physically. In the process, Nazism transformed some of the most civilized people in history into an active race of racists and of collaborators by their silence or indifference.

Nazism sought to eradicate nothing less than the Jewish part of humanity. In doing so, it brought into the world a new crime, the crime against humanity, "an attack upon human diversity as such, that is, upon a characteristic of the 'human status' without which the very words 'mankind' or 'humanity' would be devoid of meaning".[13] The Holocaust was the antithesis of the human. Hence, to his Gentile neighbour, the Jew who had survived the Holocaust became "a living reproach".[14]

The insistence on naming the Holocaust for what it was not only acknowledges the reality of the past, but also provides for the future. Once a human act makes its appearance and has been recorded in history, Arendt warns, it "stays with mankind as a potentiality long after its actuality has become a thing of the past".[15] Hence the absolute need to resist the illusion that genocide and murder are essentially the same crimes distinguished only by degree. They are not, because in genocide "an altogether different order is broken and an altogether different community is violated". The lack of this recognition would impede the emergence of a viable international penal code against genocide.[16]

Today, Holocaust deniers include those who wish to wipe Israel off the map of nations. Anti-Semites, including resurgent neo-Nazis in Europe, have more modest aims, but even they belong fully to the creed of the Nazis: Only the erstwhile opportunities and means are missing — for the time being. Umberto Eco underscores the critical need for the intelligentsia, therefore, never to legitimize the extreme right by sharing platforms that incorporate intellectuals into the right's agenda. He declares that this exclusionary stance does not detract from the liberal insistence on tolerance because, "to be tolerant, one must set the boundaries of the intolerable". It would be one thing if amateur historians tried to convince him that the Crusades were a Red Cross invention. It would be quite another thing, however, if anyone tried to make him believe that what he (like everyone else of his generation) had seen at the age of thirteen — the arrest, humiliation, and deportation of Jews — had not taken place. That attempt at denial would be intolerable. Worse, then, if the deniers should plant the seeds of doubt in young people who had not been born then. Tolerance could not mean amnesia over the fate of six million Jews and the gap that they had left in world history. "Socrates and Christ died alone," Eco says. "Two thousand years and more after their deaths, humanity is still in a state of shock, still suffering remorse for the crimes that killed them."[17]

It was in the most abnormal winter of European history that the evil normalcy of Nazism was born. With its magnificent destruction the eternal wandering of the Jew drew to a close as well. In the old Europe or in America, the Jew could have bought an old mansion and planted a garden in a bout of "anxious pastoralism", but the "dolls in the attic were not ours; the ghosts have a rented air". Characteristically, therefore, Marx, Freud, and Einstein ended their lives in exile. "The Jew has his anchorage not in place but in time, in his highly developed sense of history as personal context," Steiner declares. "Six thousand years of self-awareness are a homeland."[18]

That self-awareness was the real Jewish inheritance. It is seen in the wonderful light of empathy in "To the Land of Israel", one of the vignettes that make up *In My Father's Court*, Isaac Bashevis Singer's memoirs of a Jewish childhood in pre-World War I Warsaw. Moshe Blecher, a neighbour of the Singer family, spent every day straddling his life as a poor tinsmith and the richness of his faith in the Bible. He read Yiddish newspapers "in search only of news of Palestine and of the countries where the War of Armageddon will take place".[19] One day, he left for the Holy Land with his family. Unfortunately, once there, he could not find work — a very secular need; also, perhaps, "the dream was sweeter to him than the reality" of a Holy Land where the Turks ruled and which non-believing Jews had colonized, but where they did not live by the Torah.[20] So he returned to Warsaw. But he had left his legacy behind and, with it, the deepest part of his being. He wandered around in a state of bewilderment and talked about the Holy Land not only with adults, but with the children. He agreed with the boys in the study house that the stars in the Holy Land were as large as plums. He had heard that Lot's wife was still standing near the Dead Sea, the oxen licking the salt on her body. No, he told the boys, he had not heard Rachel weeping for her children, but a saintly man might have done so. Did they eat bread in the Holy Land, the boys asked him. If they had it, he said, they ate it.[21]

These elliptical answers reflected the believer's difficulty in reconciling the promises of faith and the unpredictability of life but, then, it was this very elusiveness that made a life of faith so astringent and rewarding. What turned the quest for the Holy Land into the defining part of Moshe Blecher's life was that it gave him a way of inhabiting the Judaic time that he had inherited. He sought the face-to-face society where, in the company of other pious believers, he could lead the Biblical life in the place where it had begun. Everywhere else — Warsaw or any other place — meant exile. So one day, Moshe Blecher returned to the Holy Land.

Moshe Blecher's final return to the Holy Land is a literary metaphor for what became Jewish reality in the decades to come, although that reality was brought to fruition by the horrors of the Holocaust. The birth of the State of Israel gave the Jew both a physical homeland and a national project in which to invest six thousand years of self-awareness. Israel placed the Jew again in charge of his destiny.

For dispossessed and displaced Palestinians, however, it was *al nakba*, the catastrophe that unsuspected destiny had wrought on them. Thus began, in the Middle East, another chapter of European history.

Postscript

Finally, in the snow-covered winter of 2009, I entered Auschwitz-Birkenau. Standing at the very spot in Birkenau where Nazi soldiers had chosen Jews arriving from all over Europe for one of two fates — immediate annihilation in the gas chambers, or a life prolonged by the agony of slave labour before an untimely death — I was struck by the ferocious irony gnawing its way through all notions of a chosen people, a chosen race, or a chosen class. Here, humans chose Jews for destruction.

A cluster of uncomfortable questions gathered in my mind. The uniqueness of the Holocaust in human history is undeniable, but is it possible to acknowledge its origins in the enormity of Nazi ideology without paying corresponding attention to the murder or brutal incarceration of non-Jewish Poles, gypsies, Soviet prisoners of war, and others? The Holocaust is as much a part of German or Polish or Hungarian history as it is of Jewish history since the collaborators, without which the Nazi project could not have grown into its enormous dimensions, were drawn from the ranks of all these groups of people. Hence, should not the Holocaust be cast in the moulds of perpetrators, collaborators, and victims rather than in terms of an ethnic history? A troubling question that accompanied this one was: Is there, in fact, a point beyond which highlighting the role of the Holocaust as the defining principle of contemporary Jewishness detracts from non-Jewish solidarity with Jews? After all, I am not a Jew, and my people were not chosen for the Holocaust. So why should I cry like a Jew for the Jews who perished? I cry because, like my Jewish brothers and sisters, I have inherited the inhumanity of human history. But can I really cry? *Can* my tears ever possess the historical agency of Jewish tears since I am not a product of Jewish time? Yet another question, driven on by contemporary urgency, followed swiftly: Would it be correct to accuse me of anti-Semitism if I criticized the actions of the Israeli state, which is a direct result of the Holocaust, towards Palestinians?

These are, of course, old questions. A book that I picked up at Auschwitz — *The Holocaust: Voices of Scholars*, a relentlessly fair exercise in academic rigour co-published by the Centre for Holocaust studies at Jagiellonian University in Cracow and the Auschwitz-Birkenau State Museum — provides fresh insights into the issues raised by such questions.[22] Auschwitz continues to pose the challenge of extending "a sense of the universe of moral obligation", Jonathan Webber writes in an essay in the book, "in which all the suffering, of all those involved, would find itself represented".[23] It is a challenge because, even leaving aside the far greater number of Jewish victims compared with other victims, Auschwitz plays asymmetrical roles in Polish and Jewish history. In the former, it speaks of the suffering of Poles at the hands of Nazis; in the latter, it attests to the "fragility of Jewish life in the diaspora".[24] Jews, for all their internal differences, "all met each other, as one people, in the gas chambers of Auschwitz".[25] Auschwitz is an "exceptionally complex case" because it symbolizes "the collective horrors of the Holocaust of the Jews" as well as the brutalization of other groups such as Sinti and Roma "with whom Jews do not necessarily feel any close sense of identification". "The fact that members of all these groups were murdered in the same place does not in itself provide them with a sense of shared destiny; on the contrary, each group tends to see its experience as unique to itself and to its own history."[26]

Striking a very different moral note, however, the eminent American historian Charles S. Maier declares that "uniqueness isn't what it was" because the "attempted genocides of recent years — in Bosnia and Rwanda — have done a great deal to take the aura of ineffability away from the murder of the Jews". Hence, it would be entirely appropriate to take a stake in an alternative historical aetiology that would locate the Holocaust, not in centuries of anti-Semitism, but in colonial wars and the "casual annihilation" of resisting tribesmen.[27] Reiterating the secularist motif in Holocaust studies, he argues that Holocaust history must be contextualized as both a Nazi utopian project and as a Jewish purgatory.[28]

Once this is done, it is possible to universalize Auschwitz and see the murder of Jews — along with that of other groups — as a defining human tragedy which, while it was carried by Jews in particular, was borne by others as well as a common burden of inhumanity. Maier's humanism contains a timeless warning against the twin dangers of essentialism and exceptionalism that bedevil efforts to create human solidarity. The Jewish part of humanity that perished at Auschwitz deserves better than the selective memory

— no matter how justified this memory is, as it is — of one people drawn from the most recent turning point in its history. Auschwitz is everything to Jewish history, but it is crucial as well to human history.

My history.

Notes

1. George Steiner, *Language and Silence: Essays 1958–1966* (Harmondsworth: Penguin Books, 1969), p. 130. The italics are in the original.
2. Hannah Arendt, *Eichmann and the Holocaust* (London: Penguin Books, 2005), p. 103.
3. Ibid., p. 31.
4. Ibid., p. 49.
5. Steiner, *Language and Silence*, op. cit., p. 15.
6. Günter Grass, "What Shall We Tell Our Children?", *On Writing and Politics 1967–1983*, translated by Ralph Manheim (San Diego, New York and London: Harcourt, 1985), p. 77.
7. Arendt, *Eichmann and the Holocaust*, op. cit., p. 58.
8. Ibid., p. 60.
9. Ibid., p. 82.
10. Ibid., pp. 84–85.
11. For an analysis of Sartre's position, see Robert Bernasconi, *Sartre* (London: Granta Books, 2006), pp. 61–69.
12. Steiner, *Language and Silence*, op. cit., p. 133.
13. Arendt, *Eichmann and the Holocaust*, op cit, pp. 92–93.
14. Steiner, *Language and Silence*, op. cit., p. 130.
15. Ibid., p. 98.
16. Ibid., pp. 97–98.
17. Umberto Eco, "Tolerance and the Intolerable", *Index on Censorship*, May/June 1994, p. 53.
18. Steiner, *Language and Silence*, op. cit., p. 131.
19. Isaac Bashevis Singer, "To the Land of Israel", *In My Father's*

Court: A Memoir (Harmondsworth: Penguin Books, 1979), p. 76.

20. Ibid., p. 78.
21. Ibid., pp. 79–80.
22. Jolanta Ambrosewicz-Jacobs, ed., *The Holocaust: Voices of Scholars* (Cracow: Centre for Holocaust Studies, Jagiellonian University, and the Auschwitz-Birkenau State Museum, 2009).
23. Jonathan Webber, "Auschwitz: Whose History, Whose Memory?", Ibid., p. 144.
24. Ibid., p. 140.
25. Ibid., p. 141.
26. Ibid., p. 138.
27. Charles S. Maier, "Holocaust Fatigue", Ibid., pp. 89–90.
28. Ibid., p. 91.

3
The Berlin Wall

loves are like empires: when the idea they are
founded on crumbles, they, too, fade away
But if to live means to exist in the eyes of those we love...
— Milan Kundera, *The Unbearable Lightness of Being*

The defeat of Nazism in 1945 was the high point of contemporary European history. The fall of the Berlin Wall in 1989 was a comparable event, although the two events belonged to different moral frames.

Jan Kott, the Polish theatre critic and theoretician who witnessed both Nazi terror and Stalinist repression, is remembered best for his daring book, *Shakespeare Our Contemporary*.[1] In his preface to the book, Peter Brook, the British director, describes how he first met Kott. It was midnight in a nightclub in Warsaw. Kott was "squashed between a wildly excited" group of students, and "we became friends at once". A beautiful girl was arrested by mistake, he leaped to her defence and, with Brook in tow, went all the way to the Polish police headquarters to try and win her release. Brook noticed that the police were calling his new friend "professor". On the way back home at four in the morning, he found out that Kott was a professor of drama.

Brook extends to Kott the ultimate compliment of calling him an Elizabethan. Like Shakespeare and his contemporaries, Kott's life is one in which "the poet has a foot in the mud, an eye on the stars, and a dagger in his hand". Shakespeare and Kott are contemporaries because it is Poland in the 1960s that comes closest to "the tumult, the danger, the intensity, the imaginativeness and the daily involvement with the social process that made life so horrible, subtle and ecstatic to an Elizabethan".[2] Much of that energy would be suppressed in the deadly 1970s, but even then, it would be possible for the protagonist of Tadeusz Konwicki's novel, *A Minor Apocalypse*, to exclaim that intellectual dissidents like him, "us cosmic castaways", are obliged "to shout through the ages into starry space". "We've become intimate with the universe."[3]

Western Europe, too, had its Elizabethan interlude, particularly in that magical year of 1968, when revolution became "the ecstasy of history".[4] "I take my desires for reality, because I believe in the reality of my desires." Now, that piece of grafitti could have come from Shakespeare, perhaps as a shred of the dream of Caliban in *The Tempest*. "When the General Assembly becomes a bourgeois theatre, bourgeois theatres must become the General Assembly." That, plausibly, could have appeared in *Julius Caesar*. "Society is a carnivorous flower." That is rather more Christopher Marlowe than Shakespeare. But the defiant declaration — "Young blood goes further than old ideals"[5] — now, that cannot but be *Hamlet*. "To forbid is forbidden." Could that be Hamlet, again, speaking to his sinning mother? "The undertakers are on strike, the dead wait for the new era, too."[6] That sounds Jacobean — John

Webster perhaps — but still in the warm aftermath of the Elizabethan period. All in all, the world dared to be young again in May 1968. The year turned the whole world into an Elizabethan stage that saw parts of the same play being acted out nearly simultaneously in Prague and Paris, in Mexico City, and Kent State University. The universal language of the new Elizabethan age was napalmed Vietnamese.

In the East Bloc, it is this Elizabethan tenor that made life sing. In *The Unbearable Lightness of Being*, the protagonist Franz's mother is Viennese, his father is French, and he himself is Swiss. Thus embodying Europe, the left-liberal academic is very much a 1968-er cast ashore the affluent society epitomized by Geneva, that safe, sanitized, and loveless boutique of a city where no political demonstrations interrupt his banally successful life as a professor. He rebels against the modern condition — really the European condition with marked French characteristics — that is immortalised in Albert Camus' formulation: "A single sentence will suffice for modern man: he fornicated and read the papers."[7] Camus is archly critical of the harmless bourgeois pursuits that remove man from the great theatres of human choice — political and moral engagement, commitment, and action — and make him a spectator and a voyeur, a coward and a veteran of every unfought war. In *Minima Moralia*, Theodor Adorno is even more scathing of modern man than is Camus. Adorno savages the very notion of bourgeois individualism, declaring that all psychology since the time of Protagoras has "elevated man by conceiving him as the measure of all things". Hence, "no measure remains for the measure of all things; lapsing into contingency, he becomes untruth".[8] The apotheosis of the individual can make society hell.

Suffering in the hellish peacefulness of Geneva, Franz is attracted to the Czech émigré painter Sabina. In her land, revolutionary illusion had faded long ago, "but where the thing he admired most in revolution remained: life on a large scale, a life of risk, daring, and the danger of death".[9] Sabina's revolt against communism is aesthetic rather than ethical. She is repelled by the ugliness of a world where ruined castles have been turned into cow sheds in an idiotic attempt to co-opt history into the egalitarian exercise, but what scandalizes her is the kitsch with which the system tries to pass off life under it as something real, genuine, and beautiful. In a never-ending attempt to rationalize and legitimate itself, totalitarian kitsch is obliged to try and banish every reality — from individualism and sexuality to doubt and irony — that reveals kitsch for the fetish and farce that it is.[10] "My enemy is kitsch, not Communism," Sabina cries.[11] Kundera is fair. "Since opinions vary," the authorial voice in the novel states, "there are various kitsches: Catholic, Protestant, Jewish, Communist, Fascist, democratic, feminist, European, American, national, international."[12]

The protagonists in Milan Kundera's novel of 1984 capture with a sad vitality the relationship between the political and sexual dimensions of life in a totalitarian society. Tereza, another Czech, muses that "loves are like empires: when the idea they are founded on crumbles, they, too, fade away".[13] That is what occurred to the socialist dream, although it had been real enough in the aftermath of Europe's experience of fascism. In this, the most luminously libidinous of novels, the insatiable bodies bouncing off each other chase after a love inscribed within the barren lay of a Czechoslovakia where politics has been sterilized of freedom, belief rid of passion. Tomas, the philandering Czech surgeon, understands that "it was a desire not for pleasure (the pleasure came as an extra, a bonus) but for possession of the world (slitting open the outstretched body of the world with his scalpel) that sent him in pursuit of women".[14] But sex is not love and a passport is not citizenship: Both require freedom in order to make meaningful commitments. What remains, in the absence of that freedom, is a negation of the individual, of his history, and of the history that gathers individuals up into what Yeats would have called the artifice of eternity. In an indictment of the futility that awaits totalitarian life in spite of its cruel control over the individual, Kundera's history does not gather up individuals. It lets them go. His history is light, light to the point of evaporating even as it takes place and vanishing forever. "History is as light as individual human life, unbearably light, light as a feather, as dust swirling into the air, as whatever will no longer exist tomorrow."[15] Hence the unbearable lightness of being.

Five unsuspected years after the publication of Kundera's novel, however, history descended on Europe with sweet vengeance.

Year of Europe

Timothy Garton Ash will go down in European history as having declared that 1989 was the best year in European history. He has moderated his assertion since. Twenty years after the fall of the Berlin Wall, he believes that 1989 was one of the best years in Europe's history (although, since he adds that he is hard pushed to think of a better year, he basically reiterates his earlier position). Perceptively as always, he remarks that 1989 was a quintessentially European year because the revolution was a truly European one. "While the French Revolution of 1789 always had foreign dimensions and repercussions, and became an international event with the revolutionary wars, it originated as a domestic development in one large country," Garton Ash writes. "The European revolution of 1989 was, from the outset, an international event — and by international I mean not just the diplomatic relations between states but also the interactions of both states and societies across borders." At any rate, 1989 was "the biggest year in world history since 1945". It ended communism in Europe, the Soviet Union, the Cold War, and the short 20th century, which had begun in 1914. It led to German reunification, "a historically unprecedented European Union stretching from Lisbon to Tallinn", the enlargement of the North Atlantic Treaty Organization (NATO), two decades of American supremacy, globalization, and the rise of Asia.[16]

What is astonishing is the peacefulness with which most of this occurred. It took World War I to destroy the Habsburg and Ottoman Empires; it took World War II to begin the dismantling of the Dutch, French, and British empires. The Cold War coincided with the entrenchment of the most modern of multinational empires. It belonged to the Soviet Union, which, displaying the instinct of the European empires it had succeeded, suppressed demands for national independence — in Berlin in 1953, Budapest in 1956, Prague in 1968, and inside the Soviet Union itself (for example in

Georgia). "The Soviet Union had alternated imperiousness — the persecution of Titoism; Stalin's purges in the satellite countries between the end of the 1940s and the beginning of the 1950s; and the Brezhnev doctrine on their limited sovereignty in the 1970s — with moments of apparent tolerance for the plurality of the 'roads to socialism.' But it had never surrendered the option of imposing the rule of imperial uniformity as much as possible."[17] That this empire, armed to the teeth with nuclear weapons, should let go of its possessions without a fight truly was remarkable.

The Berlin Wall had stood for four divisions: of Berlin, Germany, Europe, and the Cold War world. Its fall inaugurated the consecutive disappearance of the divisions. From the point of view of Europe, the Wall had signified what Milan Kundera elegantly calls the abduction of Central Europe into the Soviet sphere. "This is why the countries of Central Europe feel that the change in their destiny that occurred after 1945 is not merely a political catastrophe: It is also an attack on their civilization," Kundera wrote in 1984. "The deep meaning of their resistance is the struggle to preserve their identity — or, to put it another way, to preserve their Westernness." The Soviet Union, whose ideological self-perception was an expanded version of an already expansive Russian world view, was a natural threat to Central Europe. "Central Europe longed to be a condensed version of Europe itself in all its cultural variety, a small arch-European Europe, a reduced model of Europe made up of nations conceived according to one rule: the greatest variety within the smallest space. How could Central Europe not be horrified facing a Russia founded on the opposite principle: the smallest variety within the greatest space?"[18]

Kundera lamented that "if to live means to exist in the eyes of those we love", then Central Europe no longer existed.[19] However, what helped Central Europe was that it was not a state, but "a culture or a fate". Being imaginary, its borders had to be redrawn with each new historical situation.[20] This is what happened when the fall of the Berlin Wall created political space for the re-emergence of Mitteleuropa — a notion now shorn of connotations of German supremacy and erstwhile German justification for their control of the continent's inner core. Interwar German expansionism had given the term a bad reputation, especially in France and eastern Central European countries.[21] Now, Central Europe, liberated from the continent's political east, was free to rejoin its political west on the new European landscape created by the destruction of the ugliest edifice known to European man: the Berlin Wall.

What followed the Velvet Revolutions of 1989 in Central Europe were Georgia's Rose Revolution, Ukraine's Orange Revolution, and even Lebanon's Cedar Revolution. No longer was red the exclusive colour of revolution. Admittedly, the Balkan war revealed how bloody the break-up of empires could be, even against the backdrop of the largely peaceful Central European revolutions, but then this could be a case for differentiating between Central Europe and Eastern or South-eastern Europe. However, such differentiation should not lay the basis of cultural prejudice. "The vehemence of post-Communist populist nationalism in Catholic Slovakia, and, on the other hand, the more impressive progress towards democracy in largely Orthodox Bulgaria, should be sufficient caution against any simplistic correlation between a Western Christian past and a Western democratic future,"

Garton Ash wrote five years after the fall of the Wall.[22] What is incontrovertible is that Warsaw, Prague, or Budapest — to say nothing of Berlin — were closer to the West "for good and ill — in consumerism and crime, in politics and pornography, in a free press and unemployment, in television programmes, in the book market, yes, even in the slowly emptying churches".[23]

Ivan Klima goes to the heart of the paradox underlying the transformation. Contemptuous of totalitarianism, citizens of Warsaw Pact countries saw free Europe and the United States in "exaggeratedly attractive colours as a world of unlimited possibilities, plenty, affluence, and total freedom". At the same time, however, accustomed to the totalitarian state looking after him, the average loyal citizen felt safer living east of the Iron Curtain than he did later, in a democratic society; he had entered post-1989 Europe "culturally unprepared, with none of the antibodies against the chronic infections the value system of the market society and its mass culture concealed within itself (as indeed any human effort does)."[24] Even the intelligentsia, particularly those working in the arts and the media, fared badly because they did not fathom the nature of the transition to a democratic polity that arrived in a single package with the market economy. "Few realised that, if complete freedom came to them, it would come for everyone else as well... Instead of the dreadful but familiar enemy — the censor — came the marketplace. The marketplace has no use for dreams..."[25]

Alain Badiou argues that the fall of the Berlin Wall did not announce the arrival of a single world of freedom and democracy. Instead, the wall simply shifted: "instead of separating East and West it now divides the rich capitalist North from the poor and devastated South". Proof of this lies in the new walls that are going up all over the world: "between Palestinians and Israelis, between Mexico and the United States, between Africa and the Spanish enclaves, between the pleasures of wealth and the desires of the poor, whether they be peasants in villages or urban dwellers in *favelas, banlieues,* estates, hostels, squats and shantytowns". To unify the world, capital has to divide human existence into regions "separated by police dogs, bureaucratic controls, naval patrols, barbed wire and expulsions".[26] Even making allowance for the poetic licence with which French leftists attack capital, I fail to see how these new walls, although they are real and horrible enough, can be blamed on the fall of the Berlin Wall. What causal connection bordering on probability, to say nothing of inevitability, is there between the liberation of Central Europe, and the continuation of domination around the world?

However, more realistic, and more worrying, are fears that Europe has lost the initiative in controlling events, which it possessed for centuries. Europe is now at the mercy of what Jean Baudrillard calls "a worldwide divide which, under the ironical sign of globalization, is bringing two irreconcilable universes face to face"[27] — those of the haves and have-nots. Europe's troubles with its immigrants reveal a general milieu of alienation and anomie. Writing on France after the deaths of two Muslim teenagers caused riots in the *banlieue* of major cities in late 2005, Baudrillard declares: "This society faces a far harder test than any external threat: that of its own absence, its loss of reality. Soon it will be defined solely by the foreign bodies that haunt its periphery: those it has expelled, but who are now ejecting it from itself." It is a harsh judgement, but Baudrillard defends it by arguing that a society that "is itself disintegrating has no chance of integrating its immigrants, who are at once the products and savage analysts of its decay". He says this even if he himself is not certain that the rioters would accept integration through the traditional and mainstream remedies of employment and security. "Perhaps they consider the French way of life with the same condescension or indifference with which it views theirs," he wonders. "Perhaps they prefer to see cars burning than to dream of one day driving them." If that is so, then there is really little to be done.

Garton Ash, too, fears that European possibilities peaked in 1989, which means that Europeans in future will recall that year with a sense of nostalgia bordering on loss.

> World history — using the term in a quasi-Hegelian sense — was made in the heart of the old continent, just down the road from Hegel's old university, now called the Humboldt University... Today, world history is being made elsewhere. There is now a Café Weltgeist at the Humboldt University, but the Weltgeist [world spirit] itself has moved on. Of Europe's long, starring role on the world stage, future generations may yet say: nothing became her like the leaving of it.[28]

I hope that Garton Ash is wrong. It would be dreadful if Europe's future were to fulfil this foreboding strain of pessimism in a public intellectual whose writing, scholarly and lyrical in equal measure, did so much to call forth the very prospect of a common European home. It would be terrible if, at the end of the exertions of the Yugoslav Praxis Group, the freshness of the Prague Spring, the Ostpolitik of hope, the Helsinki Accords, Charter 77,

Antipolitics, Pope John Paul II's Polish evangelism, and Solidarity, all that remained for Europe in world affairs was to miss the train that began its journey in a Central Europe that is again at the heart of the great drama of European integration underway.

Europe does not have to miss the train. In "Archipelago Europe", Karl Schlögel writes about how

> Europe is being manufactured year by year, month by month, and day by day. Movement, which holds it together, is its basic mode... The high-speed connections turn big Europe into a small continent. The borders of individual states are crossed before the TGV really gets going. The nation state is too small for high-speed trains.

Europe is a work in progress: It is being put together again. Schlögel shows how the often contradictory mechanisms of everyday life — from reinvented cities, ports, airports, budget airlines, holidays, high-speed trains, beaches, petrol stations, hotels, love parades, the arts, and English; to plastic rubbish, Planet Moscow, and terrorist attacks — are trying to recapture the spirit of the old continent while moving on.[29]

As Galileo said, albeit in a different context: "And yet it moves."

Notes

1. Jan Kott, *Shakespeare Our Contemporary*, translated by Boleslaw Taborski (London: Routledge, 1967, second, revised edition).
2. Ibid., pp. ix–xi.
3. Tadeusz Konwicki, *A Minor Apocalypse*, translated from the Polish by Richard Lourie (New York: Vintage Books, 1984), p. 5.
4. Angelo Quattrocchi and Tom Nairn, *The Beginning of the End: France, May 1968* (London and New York: Verso, 1998), p. 39.

5. Ibid., p. 33.
6. Ibid., p. 55.
7. Albert Camus, *The Fall*, translated by Justin O'Brien (Harmondsworth: Penguin Books, 1957), p. 7.
8. Theodor Adorno, *Minima Moralia: Reflections from Damaged Life*, translated from the German by E.F.N. Jephcott (London: Verso, 1978), p. 63.
9. Milan Kundera, *The Unbearable Lightness of Being*, translated from the Czech by Michael Henry Heim (London: Faber and Faber, 1999), p. 102.
10. Ibid., pp. 246, 249.
11. Ibid., p. 252.
12. Ibid., p. 254.
13. Ibid., p. 165.
14. Ibid., p. 197.
15. Ibid., p. 220.
16. See Timothy Garton Ash, "1989 Changed the World. But where now for Europe?", *The Guardian*, 4 November 2009; and "1989!", *New York Review of Books* 56, no. 17 (5 November 2009), <http://www.nybooks.com/articles/23232>.
17. Sergio Romano, *An Outline of European History from 1789 to 1989*, translated from Italian with the assistance of Lynn Gunzberg (Oxford and New York: Berghahn Books, 1999), p. 158.
18. Milan Kundera, "The Tragedy of Central Europe", translated by Edmund White, *New York Review of Books*, 26 April 1984, reprinted in Gale Stokes, ed., *From Stalinism to Pluralism: A Documentary History of Eastern Europe Since 1945* (New York and Oxford: Oxford University Press, 1991), p. 218.
19. Ibid., p. 223.
20. Ibid., p. 220.
21. Raimo Väyrynen, "Old and New Borders in Europe", Tuomas Heikkilä, ed., *Europe 2050: Challenges of the Future, Heritage of the Past* (Helsinki: Edita, 2006), p. 129.
22. Timothy Garton Ash, "A More Civil World", *Index on Censorship* 23, no. 6 (November/December 1994): 109.

23. Ibid., p. 110.
24. Ivan Klima, "Freedom and garbage", *Index on Censorship*, Ibid., pp. 96–97.
25. Ibid., p. 98.
26. Alain Badiou, "The Communist Hypothesis", *New Left Review* 49 (January/February 2008): 38.
27. Jean Baudrillard, "The Pyres of Autumn", *New Left Review* 37 (January/February 2006): 5–7.
28. Timothy Garton Ash, "1989 Changed the World" and "1989!", op. cit.
29. Karl Schlögel, "Archipelago Europe", *eurozine*, <http://www.eurozine.com/articles/2007-10-12-schlogel-en.html>.

4
Soviets of the Mind

Comrade life
— Vladimir Mayakovsky

And yet, and yet, a global event does not mean the same thing everywhere.

Soon after the collapse of the Soviet Union in 1991, two elderly Indians were drowning their sorrows at a street-side tea stall in Calcutta. One of them was despondent and wondered how such a calamity could occur and question the inevitability of socialism. The other, dyspeptic, retorted: "Where does it say in *Das Kapital* that you and I shall be sitting here today, in this stall next to a running drain, drinking this horrible tea? If this can happen, so can that." He added: "But if the counter-revolution can occur, so can the next revolution. We are old, but the dialectic is still young." After all, Zhou Enlai had said, when asked about the impact of the French Revolution: "It's too early to tell." Had he not? Had not Roland Barthes declared that history is not a good bourgeois?[1]

This elderly Indian was taking the long view of contingency and change, but all optimism was gone. The Soviet Union had been erased from the map. A young Indian, a cousin of a friend of mine, could not handle the catastrophe and developed a mental disorder from which he suffers to this day. The two older comrades knew that they were living and would have to live in a moment of post-communist time — till, they hoped and believed, the ramparts of capital would be breached again at some unsuspected turn of the dialectic. They looked back at Soviet time with a tenderness that was almost physical.

The seven decades of world history that had followed the Bolshevik ascendancy had formed the most ambitious intellectual challenge ever posed to rump Europe. The fall of the Soviet Union represented the destruction of an alternative version of European modernity from within the Enlightenment tradition. "Communism was not a type of oriental despotism, as generations of Western scholars maintained," Gray writes. "It was an authentic continuation of a Western revolutionary tradition, and its downfall — after tens of millions of deaths were inflicted in the pursuit of its utopian goals — signalled the start of a process of de-Westernization."[2]

A non-Marxist such as me probably will never fathom the depths of belief created by serious reading of the classical texts. But even to me, it appears that at the heart of the Marxist-Leninist project was a desire that was profoundly simple: the desire to remove man's economic fear of man. This fear gone, men could be collaborators and not competitors in history. They would come together to enlarge the ambit of humanism beyond the rehearsed rituals of companionship and even intimacy that bourgeois life permitted. They would achieve a restorative world that would rehabilitate what Walter Benjamin calls the "war-disabled of competition"[3], victims of bourgeois life as an organized act of social and economic violence. The socialist project was an act of restitutive hope. It could be comprehended, therefore, only on its own terms. Benjamin, writing immediately after his visit to the Soviet Union in 1927, embodied this recuperative empathy when he said of Moscow that "every step that one takes here is on named ground".[4] Here, in Russia, "you can only see if you have already decided". "Only he who, by decision, has made his dialectical peace with the world can grasp the concrete. But someone who wishes to decide 'on the basis of facts' will find no basis in the facts."[5] Benjamin observed in the same spirit of empathy that "Bolshevism has abolished private life";[6] that there is "no knowledge and no faculty that are not somehow appropriated by collective life and made to serve it".[7] Lenin himself was a part of the project of collectivization. Benjamin looked tenderly at a portrait of the leader sitting at a table, bent over a copy of *Pravda*. Lenin's posture embodied a dialectical tension: his gaze was turned to the horizon, but "the tireless care of his heart" was turned to the moment.[8] Lenin was a part of the same dialectic that he had led his people into; he was nothing less, he was nothing more.

However, there is always a danger of the dialectic fraying. A visiting English trade union delegation averred that Lenin would be pronounced a saint one day; even as Benjamin visited Moscow, he observed that the cult of Lenin's picture was "gradually establishing its canonical forms" among his flock, hanging, for example, in the vestibule of the Kremlin's armoury just as converted heathens had erected the Cross in "formerly godless places".[9] Even in Benjamin's sympathetic rendering of Soviet socialism, it is clear that the project was looking at the slippery slope to religiosity.

The religion of Soviet socialism wilted and disappeared in merely seventy years — a month's span in the life of nations. The Kremlin failed because it tried to canonize Soviet reality. A project that had been envisaged as an act of reason was circumscribed into an article of faith; icons became fetishes. "In Communist theology the historical process occupies much the same position as the Holy Spirit does in Christianity: an omnipotent power that co-operates with the human will but is not dependent on it," Northrop Frye writes.[10]

In its exertions, however, the Communist Church could not replicate the Catholic Church. The Reformation had occurred when the sale of papal indulgences had exposed the depth of the Church's worldly corruption. But the Catholic Church remained, and fought back with the Counter-Reformation. With the Second Vatican Council, Rome of the 1960s sought to heal the schism between the Churches of East and West in 1054, and the rifts caused by the Reformation. Vatican II demonstrated a healthy awareness of the frailty of even God-driven institutions in a world of mortals, and therefore the need for reform.[11] Beyond and above these reforms, the Catholic Church survived its own convulsions chiefly because it promised mortals heaven in the next life if they would abide by its strictures in this life. Meanwhile, it allowed them to be human, for example, to laugh, so long as they laughed outside the Church. Mikhail Bakhtin demonstrates, in his magnificent study of laughter as a motif of Western civilization, how the Church moved beyond early Christianity's condemnation of laughter, the prerogative of plebes in the age of the Ancients, and allowed mime, jests, and taunts to emerge as social forms that ran parallel to canonized ritual and etiquette.[12] The Renaissance democratized laughter to the extent that it became a "completely loud, marketplace frankness". Laughter revealed the hidden and unspoken side of the world that refused to fit into prevailing forms of philosophy.[13] By contrast, Bakhtin had to struggle against a humourless Soviet orthodoxy to have his book accepted. It did not help that Anatoly Lunacharsky, the Commissar of Enlightenment in the 1930s, had organized a special official committee to study satiric genres.[14] Prohibited from laughing over their fate after having been forbidden to cry over it, most of the Soviet flock slipped into despondency. The Kremlin looked on, unsmilingly.

The Kremlin could not do what the Vatican did. Unlike the Catholic Church, which had all eternity at its disposal, the Communist Church, purveyor of secular mysteries, had to deliver tangible results within the lifespan of generations. It could not. Instead, the Kremlin became an office of imperial obsessions, presiding over the vast, repressive, and expanding bureaucratization of life in the lands and satellites of the Soviet state. With his crass and ruthless personification of the Communist Party of the Soviet Union (CPSU), Stalin went from being the chief priest of Marxism-Leninism to the godhead of the Soviet Church. His party purges, show trials, assassinations, and mass exiles to Siberian prison camps claimed not only rivals such as Leon Trotsky, but the very idea of a socialism of free choice and critical belief. Those excesses — which became normal occurrences in the hyperreality of the Stalinist age — killed any possibility of a socialist democracy.

Stalin's successors settled for less grand and murderous visions, but the 20th Congress of the CPSU failed to achieve the soul-searching on which Vatican II would embark. These successors — stodgy bishops of mediocrity whom the Party had catapulted into history — could not turn the Soviet Church back into a congregation, let alone one made up of the dissenting and the free. Instead, the dramatic invasions of Hungary in 1956 and Czechoslovakia in 1968 showed how vulnerable the Soviet Church had become to its imperial overreach. It needed to protect its ideological borders, not through the force of ideas, as would be natural, but through the might of the military. The arrogance of power without reflected the decay of legitimacy within. Benjamin had warned in 1927 that there was one indispensable condition for the health of the Soviet socialist republic, "that never (as one day happened even to the Church) should a black market of power be opened". "Should the European correlation of power and money penetrate Russia, too, then perhaps not the country, perhaps not even the Party, but Communism in Russia would be lost".[15] This is precisely what occurred, of course. It was a matter of time before even the Party stopped believing its lies. Then came the time to stop telling them.

When the Berlin Wall crumbled, the restless dioceses — East Germany, Poland, Hungary, and all — headed westwards. Mikhail Gorbachev's Reformation emptied the Soviet Church. Boris Yeltsin put the Church itself up for sale. Rome had survived the Holy Roman Empire. The Kremlin, too, survived the bankrupt Holy Soviet Empire, but shorn of the socialist religion.

At the fall of the Soviet Union, my mind went back, somewhat incongruously, to Giovannino Guareschi's *Mondo piccolo: Don Camillo*, that profoundly delightful collection of tales of unwilling coexistence. The colourful parish priest of "a quaint, Northern Italian Everyvillage" is forced to deal with his town's newly-elected, post-war communist government. The fiesty Don Camillo proves to be more than a match for his foe, the formidable Mayor Peppone, largely because of the guidance of Christ on the altar Cross. The reader can hear both sides of the conversation between Christ and Don Camillo. The priest seeks to justify his desire to give a muscular reply to the baiting he suffers at the hands of Peppone and his supporters, but Christ's tender and cheerful love hovers over both priest and communist, and disarms Don Camillo's desire for revenge. "The Don Camillo tales were fable-like," Welbourne writes, "yet they reflected a very real situation; they wickedly satirized their Red target, yet they displayed a genuine tenderness on the part of the author toward all of his characters."[16] The problem today is that, with Peppone's world in ideological disarray, Christ no longer has an atheist mayor at whom to gaze tenderly.

The disappearance of the Union of Soviet Socialist Republics (USSR) freed Marxism-Leninism to resume a theoretical journey that had been hijacked by the harshness and darkness of Soviet reality. That is for the future — perhaps. For the time being, however, the secular verities of revolutionary socialism have vanished. The story of Marxism has left the legacy that all great periods of history do: it has become literature. Marshall Berman predicts that the wonderful gallery of humans portrayed in *Das Kapital* has "a life that will outlive capitalism itself".[17] Marx's literary metaphors have passed into the moral imagination, where the division of labour produces the scattered limbs of Orpheus, and the pains of Dante's *Inferno* fall short of the hellish diseases caused by the raw handling of phosphorus in Victorian match factories.[18] There, in that literary repertoire, the political metaphors rest, tired but immutable, for what is wrought by the mind lives on in the mind, impervious to the accidents of time and the exigencies of place.

Notes

1. Barthes, *Mythologies*, op. cit., p. 77.
2. John Gray, *Enlightenment's Wake* (London and New York: Routledge Classics, 2007), p. xiv.
3. Walter Benjamin, *Reflections*, translated by Edmund Jephcott (New York: Schocken Books, 1986), p. 135.
4. Ibid., p. 99.
5. Ibid., pp. 97–98.
6. Ibid., p. 108.
7. Ibid., p. 107.
8. Ibid., p. 130.
9. Ibid.
10. Northrop Frye, *The Modern Century* (Toronto: Oxford University Press, 1967), p. 32.
11. <http://vatican2voice.org/>.
12. Mikhail Bakhtin, *Rabelais and His World*, translated by Hélène Iswolsky (Bloomington: Indiana University Press, 1984), pp. 73–74.
13. Ibid., p. 271.
14. Krystyna Pomorska, "Foreword", in Ibid., p. xi.
15. Benjamin, *Reflections*, op. cit., p. 117.
16. <http://home.comcast.net/~doncamillo/authorinfo.htm>.
17. Marshall Berman, *Adventures in Marxism* (London and New York: Verso, 1999), p. 81.
18. S.S. Prawer, *Karl Marx and World Literature* (Oxford: Oxford University Press, 1978), pp. 332, 339.

5
The Secular Soul

And yet it moves
— Galileo Galilei

The Quai d'Orsay invited a dozen Asian journalists to savour the feel of France in the summer of 2004. On a free day during the trip, my tourist map of Paris led me to to the Church of Saint-Germain-des-Prés. Many religious observances, whatever the faith, are almost funereal in nature. People attending them are on their best behaviour, as if they are prepared to drop dead and be judged eternally, immediately after the onerous ceremonies are over. But this church, consecrated in 1163, is different. Here — as in the thirteenth-century Cathédrale de Chartres, which, too, I visited — humans are not quite a part of God's family. Instead, the Almighty has been co-opted into an extended human family. And that family was having a roaring party in church when this tourist dropped in.

In Saint-Germain-des-Prés, children played on their parents' laps while priests spoke of the Heavenly Father. One earth-based father had his attention diverted by his little son, who kissed him repeatedly. Close by, on the floor, sat a toddler. He had been propitiated with a set of toys. When he grew tired of them, he made his displeasure known, loudly and forcefully. His mother, who had been focusing on Mass, turned to him in one effortless movement from Heaven to earth and soothed him. She then returned to her prayers and he to his toys. The French, it appeared, do not believe in scolding their children, especially in the presence of the Heavenly Father.

A man was singing traditional, devotional songs. Training had made his voice crystal clear, but what divine training was it that made the voice tactile to the soul? How French, is it not, that enigmatic dictim of the American Don Marquis — that you don't have to have a soul unless you really want one?[1] Here, you really wanted a soul. The children fell silent; it was the adults' turn to have tears well up in their eyes.

When it came to queuing for Holy Communion, all Heaven broke loose. A girl of about eight sashayed up to the priest, who gave her a wafer. She asked for one more. Laughing, he made a face at her and pretended to scold her, whereupon she ran away in mock hurt. Such mirth in the House of God? Surely, then, God has a sense of humour. Why, He might even be French, I wondered to myself as I wrenched myself away from the party.

I made my way to the Cathédrale Notre-Dame de Paris. An elderly woman was begging at the entrance. Two teenage girls were entering the cathedral. One recognized her and struck up a conversation. The woman stopped begging and ignored everyone. The girl kept chatting: For her, God could wait. For the first time in my life, I waited five eternal minutes to drop a paltry coin into a beggar's cup overflowing with cheer.

When I left France, it was I who had received far, far more than I had given, for here, in the secular heart of Europe, I had witnessed the religion of a free people. It was that freedom that, in turn, helped preserve Europe as a secular bastion in a dicey world.

Against Confessionalism

The dissolution of the Soviet Union fuelled a bout of philosophical triumphalism in Francis Fukuyama, whose *The End of History and The Last Man* encapsulated the spirit of what appeared to be a post-Hegelian age. Yet, it was Samuel Huntington's *The Clash of Civilizations* that proved to be more prescient than missives about the death of history. The missive, much as Mark Twain's quip about news of his own demise, was slightly exaggerated.

I do not know whether Osama bin Laden ever read Huntington, but he certainly turned parts of the Harvard academic's thesis into nightmarish practice. The destruction of the Twin Towers was both a physical and a metaphysical attack on New York, on America, on the idea of America, and on the West that, in the terrorist imagination, is implicated in the idea of America.[2] "The Twin Towers, filled with people of all races, nationalities, and creeds, working in the service of global capitalism, represented everything that was hateful to the holy warrior about the greatest modern City of Man."[3]

Paradoxically, Osama's war on the West has its roots in the West itself.[4] It was the West that spawned what Ian Buruma and Avishai Margalit call Occidentalism, "the dehumanizing picture of the West as painted by its enemies".

Occidentalism was born in Europe before it was carried to other parts of the world. "The West was the source of the Enlightenment and its secular, liberal offshhots, but also of its frequently poisonous antidotes," they write in *Occidentalism*. Osama took off from where those antidotes had ended, with the essential difference that, whereas Western Occidentalism had been an intellectual exercise largely, his murderous war on the West was a real one.

Look at how spectacularly he has failed on two fronts. First, his boast was that the West, which loves life, would not be able to fight his warriors, who love death. In taunting the West, he joined a long list of Occidentalists such as Werner Sombart, Oswald Spengler, and Ernst Jünger, who found contemptible "the cowardly bourgeois habit of clinging to life, of not wishing to die for great ideals, of shying away from violent conflict and denying the tragic side of life".[5] But the West has fought back: Osama's caliphate remains but a violent dream without the remotest chance of creating a unified Muslim camp of warriors stretching from Riyadh to Riau. Second, the West has fought back without falling into the trap that Osama set for it: to turn the West against its best values and make it unleash a reign of terror on Muslims in its midst. The aftermath of 9/11 belied the scale of the attack that Osama had mounted that day. In America and elsewhere in the West, there was no mass killing of Muslims in retaliation, no mass deportation of Muslim foreigners, no mass incarceration in camps, no mass expulsions to refugee camps. Everyone — Muslim, Christian and Jew alike — took refuge in the civility of the West as a sanctuary of human liberty and security. Of course, no such benediction awaited the unfortunates sent to Guantanamo Bay and Abu Ghraib.

However, the deepest values and traditions of the West have prevailed. The West stayed true to its love of life.

One reason for the West's ability to stay the course is its historical achievement in having produced secular societies that exist in stark contrast to confessional societies. In confessional societies, membership of the political and social order rests on public confessions of faith. Confessional societies make citizenship a secondary function of their primary function — the state playing God — with the citizen believing in the state's self-vested role or, more likely, agreeing to play along because it is politic to do so. The idea that faith presupposes a self, and that selfhood in turn presupposes a private sphere in which the citizen can refuse to subscribe to a particular religion or to any religion, is anathema to the rationale of such societies.

The West exhibits many varieties of secularism. In France, secularism means keeping religion out of the state. In the United States, secularism means keeping the state out of religion. In Britain, where the monarch is the head of the Church of England, secularism is ensured through constitutional safeguards and, no less importantly, through habits of the heart. What is common to all these societies, however, is the idea that an individual's religion, or absence or religion, is a matter of private choice for her or him although, of course, he or she may display that choice in the public sphere by joining congregations, participating in festivals, observing rituals, and so on — or by abstaining from them. The state cannot invade the citizen's private sphere to determine religious choice, let alone compel the citizen to abide by a religious choice that the state has made. The state cannot play God. Moses Finley makes this point with a simplicity that even a child can understand. "Anyone who holds that the proper function of the state is to bring about the moral perfection of its citizens is playing with very dangerous weapons," he writes in *Aspects of Antiquity.* "If he then anchors his moral judgements in absolute truths, whether they are called Ideal Forms or God, his conviction will lead him, if he is rigorous enough, to believe that he has the right and the duty to impose these absolutes on others for their own good, as in Plato's Republic or the Holy Inquisition or Calvin's Geneva or Orwell's *Nineteen Eighty-Four.* Absolute truths can neither be questioned nor challenged nor flouted."[6] Instead, the good life of politics consists, not in the search for finality, but in the building of communities worth living in, out of "the crooked timber of humanity", that inestimable choice of title for Isaiah Berlin's classic contribution to political philosophy.[7] The need to proceed through trial and error in an imperfect world returns the Western mind over and over again, in John Gray's formulation, to "the realities of political life, which have to do with balancing competing claims of similar validity, finding a *modus vivendi* among forms of life that are irreconcilable, and mediating conflicts that can never be resolved".[8] That idea of mediating conflicts which cannot be resolved is redolent of the fundamental recognition in secularism that issues of faith cannot be resolved by the state, whose proper role is to preserve a level playing field among faith communities — or faithless communities.

The Provenance of Europe

Europe is critical to the secular course of Western history; indeed, secularism is critical to the course of European history. There is a happy irony in the provenance of the secular given how drenched in religion European history is.

Europe was born of the union of the Judeao-Christian and Graeco-Roman worlds. When the Middle Ages incorporated the history, culture, and politics of the classical, pagan world into the Judeao-Christian framework, they shifted the very centre of gravity of world history.[9] Moses Finley tends to dismiss the veracity of the chronological incorporation, which is inherent in the great question of whether Homer or Moses came first.[10] However, he re-emphasizes the Greek, Roman, and Judeao-Christian roots of Europe. "The Romanization of western Europe, for which the Augustan imperial settlement was essential, was one factor that eventually made the idea of Europe possible." The empire's eastern half, which was not fundamentally Romanized, broke away from both Rome and Europe, "but it produced and exported to Europe a second binding factor, a common and exclusive religion.[11]

The Middle Ages were reinvigorated by the rediscovery of the Greek classics, which had survived the fall of the Roman Empire and the collapse of order in Europe through the protective translations of Arab Muslim and Jewish interpreters such as Avicenna, Averroes, and Moses Maimonides. Housed in the great university libraries of Baghdad, Cairo, Toledo, and Cordoba, they received a second lease of life. The rediscovery of Aristotle's works in Arabic ignited a culture war in the European High Middle Ages that would transform the Latin West from a provincial region into the heartland of an expansive global civilization.[12] Departing from the Neoplatonic tradition that Saint Augustine had derived through Plotinus and that had come to hold sway over mediaeval minds, Saint Thomas Aquinas achieved his great synthesis between Aristotle's metaphysical and epistemological teachings, and Christian theology. A capacity to absorb new information and respond to new challenges marked mediaeval Europe, which went from being a Mediterranean backwater to the world's foremost economic, political, and military power in the early modern era.[13]

How far did the Middle Ages create modern Europe and its emphasis on the secular? In a recent intervention, Tuomas Heikkilä warns against making too much of the era as the template for today's European Union, for example, by exulting over the fact that the borders of the original member-states of the European Economic Community corresponded broadly with those of the Carolingian Empire in the early ninth century.[14] The Middle Ages lend themselves too easily to nationalist and chauvinist propaganda when in truth mediaeval Europe was at best a tentative and provisional project that was by no means a "proto-Europe".[15] For one thing, the Roman Empire, the Byzantine Empire, the Carolingian Empire, the Holy German Empire, and the Russian Empire did not last all that long; for another thing, the Church, the universal empire, was splintered into rival movements.[16] None of these institutions functioned and lasted long enough to create the basis for the political and cultural unity that they saw as Europe's ultimate destination. Europe included vast pagan areas before 1300; this fact means that the continent can properly be termed Christian only after that date.[17] True, *Respublica Christiana* was a reality: It was through religion that the Latin world in western Europe and the Greek world in eastern Europe succeeded in bringing Germanic, Slavic, and other heathens into a common framework of values that are called European today.[18] But the first "European" expansion, conducted by missionaries in the Early and High Middle Ages, did not prevent religious strife from tearing Europe apart at the end of the Middle Ages. The reformation of the early sixteenth century broke the religious unity of Western Christendom itself. Even when there was no conflict, Heikkilä notes, there was confrontation of another kind. In mediaeval Europe, the Christian God and saints "hovered over both the universal and the local levels of existence", with pagan spirits exercising some local influence — resulting in contention between the local and the universal seen plentifully in the European Union as well.[19] The mediaeval exercise in Europe-making was weakened by the incapacity of the temporal and ecclesiastical establishments to really work together.

True. Yet, there is a tangible sense in which modern Europe has emerged out of the religious contests and confrontations that connect the religious life of the classical ages to that of mediaeval times. Out of the coexistence of the Pauline Church and Roman law, the notion of secularism, or the separation of Church and State, had been born, with each source of legitimacy being accorded its proper, if contested, realm. The Reformation, in which Luther made every man his own priest, confirmed this awesome split; the rest of European history serves to affirm the happy heresy in its essentials. The subversive cosmology of Copernicus, Kepler, and Galileo, part of the expanding boundaries of humanism in the Renaissance, provided the intellectual framework for the Reformation to consolidate the gains of secularism. Europe elevated the sovereign nation-state to the role of key actor in global politics; that achievement, which reflected a decline in religious sentiment in affairs within and between states, represented nothing less than the secularization of international relations. When, following the Thirty Years' War, Europe produced the Peace of Westphalia in 1648, it laid the template of the Westphalian system of international relations that exists to this day.

This early *Pax Europa* announced at Westphalia provided a context for Enlightenment *philosophes* to turn Europe from an idea to a world idea. Secularism was embedded in that transition. Although cosmology had reduced the earth's status to that of one planet among many, and although the work of seventeenth-century anthropologists and philosophers obliged *Homo Europeensis* to acknowledge the history of classical-Christian civilization as only an account of "one of the more fortunate branches of a numerous family",[20] Europe fought back with its values. In John Gray's sombre ruminations, the Enlightenment project was the foundational initiative in Western modernism and the West's chief legacy to the rest of the world. The "project of giving human institutions a claim on reason that has universal authority" pointed to a "universal convergence on a rationalist civilization as its *telos*".[21] That modernist project continued the classical and mediaeval quest for universalism. The pre-modern world view, held by both Aristotelianism and its Thomistic rendition, had averred that human moral categories could be used to "track the structure of things in the world" and that "human reason reflects in microcosm the order of the cosmos". The modern period rejected or marginalized the metaphysical and religious beliefs of the classical and Christian eras, but it secularized or naturalized the moral categories or hopes of those eras, now through humanist doctrines of autonomous reason, historical progress, and so on.[22] Out of this keenly fought struggle for the modern, which emerged from the passionate engagement between religion and philosophy, appeared Europe's legacy of secularism.

The Hebraic and the Hellenic

Europe's wariness of confessionalism is seen in its literary traditions. They bear the pagan imprint, at least partially, of Matthew Arnold's distinction between Hebraism and Hellenism. "The uppermost idea with Hellenism is to see things as they really are; the uppermost idea with Hebraism is conduct and obedience," he writes.[23] While Hebraism "seizes upon certain plain, capital intimations of the universal order, and rivets itself, one may say, with unequalled grandeur of earnestness and intensity on the study and observance of them, the bent of Hellenism is to follow, with flexible activity, the whole play of the universal order, to be apprehensive of missing any part of it, of sacrificing one part to another, to slip away from resting in this or that intimation of it, however capital".[24] Erich Auerbach illustrates the distinction in his majestic *Mimesis*. Homer delights in physical existence; the heroes of his poems "bewitch us and ingratiate themselves to us until we live with them in the reality of their lives", Auerbach declares.[25] By contrast, the jealous world of the Old Testament is not satisfied with claiming that its reality is historically true: It demands that its reality be accepted as the only one. Homer's stories court and flatter the reader: The Scripture seeks to subject the reader and, if he refuses to be subjected, treats him as a rebel.[26]

I do not agree entirely with this critique of Hebraism. As a non-Christian and a non-Jew, I read the Book of

Job, the Psalms of David, or Ecclesiastes without having obligations of belief thrust on me. I read them as literature. As literature, those parts of the Old Testament *sing* for me, and they sing no less than *Antigone* and *Medea* do. Perhaps it was the Christian framework within which Arnold thought that forced him to choose between the credal appeal of the Old Testament and the literary appeal of Hellenic works. For someone outside that framework to begin with, there is no choice to be made. Nevertheless, Arnold has a point. The Hebraic and the Hellenic exercised distinct pulls on Westerners in his time, the overwhelming majority of whom were practising Christians or observant Jews.

Arnold is careful to qualify his argument by noting that both the Hebraic and the Hellenic strains are present forever, interact closely with each other, and help to shape the Western imagination. However, in literature, as in other fields of activity, the drift of the secular West today is intensely Hellenic. This is one result of the fact that, having taken up the dropped baton of the Greeks, the Renaissance raced into a world where man became "a less passive creature, less the subject of revelation and more himself the one who revealed".[27] Man sought freedom, not *within* faith, but *from* faith, if he so chose. Erwin Panofsky writes of the "world of difference" between the mediaeval freedom to accept or reject the Grace of God, and man's "freedom to choose between his own, self-generated impulses" that came to fruition in the Renaissance. The mediaeval idea of freedom is captured in a drawing of a man torn between an angel and a devil; the Renaissance idea of freedom is illustrated by a man choosing between Pleasure and Virtue.[28] The idea of creation, which had been restricted to the realm of God, now entered the domain of man. Panofsky declares that

the inhabitants of the twentieth century — "surrounded by
hats 'created' by Lili Dache, lipsticks 'created' by Helena
Rubinstein, freshman courses in 'creative writing' and
progressive schools providing 'creative play periods,'"
— cannot comprehend easily "what it meant to transfer to
human production the very verb", "creation", that St. Thomas
insisted could not be applied "to any action other than that of
God". "But that is precisely what the Renaissance did."[29]
    Man's secular creation of the world around him
continues uninterrupted in Europe. "I take my desires for
reality, because I believe in the reality of my desires" — so
read the sign in a Sorbonne amphitheatre during the May
1968 upheaval that shook Gaullist France to its foundations.[30]
That graffiti would have been meaningless in a Hebraic
culture where desires are by their nature prohibited from
being real. "We interrupt the work of the gods,/hasty and
inexperienced beings of the moment," Constantine Cavafy,
the most classical of the modern Greek poets, announces.[31]
The Hebraic mind would understand the second line
instinctively: It requires the Hellenic imagination to dare
pen the first line, at which the Hebraic mind would squirm,
confronted with a monstrous sacrilege.

The Ironic Sense of Life

Secularism has a price. It strives to transcend both the
Hellenic and the Hebraic lessons of life. The tragedy of the
ancient Greeks exulted in the fact that, in Hellene, the gods
lived and played among men. However, man was insecure
and lonely among these frivolous gods, who might not be
around when needed. The Old Testament reassured men

by placing God outside *their* frivolous arena, but it failed to assure God-left man that He was still around to care for him. The Book of Job could not have been written had it been otherwise.

The Advent of Christ changed both the Hellenic and the Hebraic worlds irrevocably. Here and now was God made flesh. With his crucifixion, Christ made his death the life of his believers. In their lives, they had access to him. Their tragedies were his tragedies as well. Christian tragedy was the length of time that men spent waiting for the redemption promised in Christ. The flux of days was worthwhile because all days moved towards him.

Secularism destroyed that waiting. In a fundamental critique of secularism, Miguel de Unamuno bemoans the decline of the tragic sense of life in the West. The Renaissance, the Reformation, and the Scientific Revolution destroyed the tragic imagination and "brought us a new Inquisition: that of science and culture, which turns its weapons of ridicule and contempt against whoever does not submit to its orthodoxy".[32] Marlowe's Faustus and Goethe's Faust show the folly and the price of the unbridled desire for mastery over the natural world — the mandate of the new secular science. Spanish Catholicism — "a political economy of the eternal, that is, of the divine"[33] — blocks the Faustian way, but Cervantes, trying to recover what Faust lost to the secular world — the very tragic sense of life — can do no better than turn Don Quixote into a tragicomic hero.

Secularism snaps the tension between the here and the hereafter. The devil usually comes to "those who have everything and are bored with it"; in a "society of the accepted and the adequately fed",[34] comfort and ease are the greatest temptations because they lead ultimately to nothing but man's alienation from the deepest springs of his being. Progress is no antidote to alienation. When all is said and done, progress is but "a social projection of the individual's sense of the passing of time". The individual himself "is not progressing to anything except his own death".[35]

The tragic sense gives depth to the life of nations: Its disappearance vulgarizes them. José Ortega y Gasset lays out explicitly the political implications of the loss of the tragic sense of life. He warns that the entry of mass-man into the historical process — produced by the tripling of the European and American population within a hundred years of the modern period — is replacing an aristocracy of excellence with the commonness of inertia. And mass-man is dangerous because "his actions are devoid of the note of inevitability": Men "play at tragedy because they do not believe in the reality of the tragedy which is actually being staged in the civilised world".[36] Ortega's politics resonate with de Unamuno's religiosity. However, in an emphatic repudiation of a tragic sense of life born out of a religious ethic, Friedrich Nietzsche restates the case for secularism. He insists on the assertion that "both art and life depend wholly on the laws of optics, on perspective and illusion; both, to be blunt, depend on the necessity of error".[37]

The epic, heroic, chivalric, and the tragic modes of thinking kept Europe company from mediaeval times to the early modern. One by one, they fell by the way. In their place, the ironic mode arrived, and is now in full bloom. This mode is predicated on the realization that, because there is no perfect or final form of government or society, what matters in the passage of time is its direction, not its destination. Ironic and secular societies, so profoundly European, are still a mercy because they reduce the urge to kill or die for the tribe, nation, state, or faith to pave the way for a chialistic future. The climate of opinion originating at Westphalia — which banished religion to the outskirts of international politics — is encapsulated in the playful political agnosticism of John Byrom's lines: "God bless the King, I mean the Faith's Defender;/ God bless — no harm in blessing — the Pretender;/ But who Pretender is, or who is King, / God bless us all — that's quite another thing." Ironic societies represent life, not death. By their very existence, they challenge confessional societies that, in their most virulent form, spawn suicide bombers who are willing to die in killing others, even if those others do not wish to kill them.

Precisely here, however, lie the limitations of the ironic sense of life. What confessional absolutisms demand of their followers — death for others or oneself — ironic man finds outlandish. But if the desire for life and freedom and individuality is so strong as to domesticate the ability to die in defence of the liberties that make society human, ironic man might have a few problems down the road with keeping his ironic society alive. This problem is evident already, for example, in the demilitarization of life in Europe. No European is willing to die defending a phase of history that will die anyway. He might serve in the military, but that is a profession and not a religious vocation. He does not serve history. In any case, only a small part of society joins the military. To the modern European, the state has no purchase on human life.

That is fine — or is it? Not to be willing to die also
has its problems. One person's life demands that someone
else protect it. Who will? Who should? Why should he in
societies marked by what Roger Scruton calls the "culture
of repudiation" that has invaded the West? This culture
demeans the defenders of freedom by devaluing what they
defend, through the rejection of family values; the excesses
of Western, academic feminism; the ubiquitous rise of
political correctness; and the growth of multiculturalism.
This culture is marked as well by the tendency of rights-
based arguments, emanating now from demands based
on group rights, to flourish at the expense of reciprocity.
Arguing against this culture, Scruton strikes a conservative
but realistic chord when he remarks that if "*all* that Western
civilization offers is freedom, then it is a civilization bent
on its own destruction"[38] because man "cannot live by rights
alone".[39] That is a timeless statement; what gives it urgency
is a facet of life today that Scruton focuses on. This is, that
modern political society reinforces the need for a community
of outlook because, unlike the face-to-face society of the
Greek *polis*, a modern democracy "is perforce a society of
strangers", and "the successful democracy is the one where
strangers are expressly included in the web of obligation".[40]
Defending modern society is therefore more onerous than
defending the *polis*. Combine the two parts of Scruton's
argument and its import is clear. If society is repudiated, and
if even that repudiated society is but a society of strangers,
why should the modern soldier be willing to lay down his
life for what the intelligentsia is telling him is essentially
a chimera?

It is a sobering thought. I realized how sobering it is
several years ago. I was at Eden Hall, the residence of the

British High Commissioner to Singapore, for a reception to mark the Queen's Birthday. Moved by the sombre lowering of the colours at dusk to the accompaniment of loyal Gurkha bugles, I asked the man next to me whether he would die for his country. "Good question," he said. "Let me ask my wife." He asked her whether she would die for Britain. "Actually, I'd rather live, darling," she said. "I love parties. Like this one. Now, where did I leave the beer?" Attention reverted thereupon to the beer and the fish and chips wrapped in newspapers. A Brit conceivably might die in a fight over fish and chips, but which Brit in her right mind would want to die for a place in news destined to wrap fish and chips that *others* would eat? Who?

The problem remains, therefore. Secular and ironic societies, humane products of the life-loving West, are called upon to protect themselves from the death-loving outriders of confessional states and tribes. How they can defend themselves, without sacrificing the values that make them worth defending in the first place, is a question the answer to which will determine Europe's fate in an uneasy world in the years to come.

Notes

1. Cited in Clifford Geertz, *Islam Observed: Religious Development in Morocco and Indonesia* (Chicago and London: The University of Chicago Press, 1971), p. 100.
2. Ian Buruma and Avishai Margalit, *Occidentalism: The West in the Eyes of its Enemies* (New York: Penguin, 2005), p. 14.
3. Ibid., p. 21.
4. Ibid., pp. 5–6.
5. Ibid., p. 54.
6. M.I. Finley, *Aspects of Antiquity: Discoveries and Controversies*

(New York and London, Penguin Books, Second Edition, 1977), op. cit., p. 85.

7. Isaiah Berlin, *The Crooked Timber of Humanity*, Henry Hardy, ed. (Princeton: Princeton University Press, 1998).

8. John Gray, *Enlightenment's Wake*, op. cit., p. 13.

9. Maurice Keen, "Mediaeval Ideas of History", in *The Mediaeval World*, David Daiches and Anthony Thorlby, general eds. (London: Aldus Books, 1973), pp. 298–99.

10. Finley, *Aspects of Antiquity*, op. cit., p. 167.

11. Ibid., p. 199.

12. Richard E. Rubinstein, *Aristotle's Children: How Christians, Muslims, and Jews Rediscovered Ancient Wisdom and Illuminated the Middle Ages* (Orlando: Harvest Books, 2004), pp. 4–5.

13. Tuomas Heikkilä, "The Middle Ages and the Birth of Europe", in Tuomas Heikkilä, ed., *Europe 2050*, op. cit., p. 57.

14. Ibid., p. 59.

15. Ibid., p. 40.

16. Ibid., p. 41.

17. Ibid., p. 44.

18. Ibid., p. 48.

19. Ibid., pp. 49–50.

20. Norman Hampson, *The Enlightenment* (Harmondsworth: Penguin Books, 1968), p. 27.

21. Gray, *Enlightenment's Wake*, op. cit., p. 97.

22. Ibid., p. 227.

23. Matthew Arnold, *Culture and Anarchy and Other Writings*, Stefan Collini, ed. (Cambridge: Cambridge University Press, 1993), p. 127.

24. Ibid., p. 128.

25. Erich Auerbach, *Mimesis: The Representation of Reality in Western Literature*, translated from the German by Willard R. Trask (New Jersey: Princeton University Press, 1968), p. 13.

26. Ibid., pp. 14–15.

27. Michael Levey, *Early Renaissance* (Harmondsworth: Penguin, 1967), p. 112.

28. Erwin Panofsky, "Artist, Scientist, Genius: Notes on the 'Renaissance-Dammerung'", *The Renaissance: Six Essays* (New York: Harper Torchbooks, 1962), pp. 167–69.
29. Ibid., p. 171.
30. Angelo Quattrocchi and Tom Nairn, *The Beginning of the End*, op. cit., p. 26.
31. Constantine P. Cavafy, "Interruption", *The Complete Poems of Cavafy*, translated by Rae Dalven (San Diego, New York and London: Harvest, 1976), p. 12.
32. Miguel de Unamuno, *The Tragic Sense of Life in Men and Nations*, translated by Anthony Kerrigan (New Jersey: Princeton University Press, 1972), p. 327.
33. Ibid., pp. 347–48.
34. Frye, *The Modern Century*, op. cit., p. 24.
35. Ibid., p. 35.
36. José Ortega y Gasset, *The Revolt of the Masses*, anonymous translator (New York and London: W.W. Norton, 1957), pp. 104–05.
37. Friedrich Nietzsche, *The Birth of Tragedy and The Genealogy of Morals*, translated by Francis Golffing (New York: Doubleday Anchor Books, 1956), pp. 10, 11.
38. Roger Scruton, *The West and the Rest: Globalization and the Terrorist Threat* (London and New York: Continuum, 2002), p. viii.
39. Ibid., p. 68.
40. Ibid., p. 53.

6
The Leopard's Italy

On a conducted tour of Italy undertaken on the cheap in the summer of 2004, my family and I travelled by coach. We generally stayed in little hotels tucked into city outskirts, where people and places could not be bothered to put on a show for tourists. Our ten-day tour took us to Rome, the Vatican City, Pisa, Milan, Verona, Venice, Florence, Assisi, Pompeii, Sorrento, Naples, and Capri. We did see a bit of Italy. The patrician north swept by on the whiff of an arrogance manufactured in some perfumery of the Roman Empire. But in Florence and Rome, we also saw men and women who seemed to have stepped right out of the canvases of the Masters. Is that Caravaggio's Narcissus, reduced now to producing sketches for tourists? How obscene it is for a foreigner to come to Italy and be consumed by his own beauty! Look, Italians are so beautiful that the Renaissance came here for a visit and stayed on as art forever. Foolish tourists, be gone.

By the time we were in the south, we met people. In Sorrento, for the princely sum of 9.80 euros spent in a provision shop, I got to chat with the matriarch. She spoke in Italian and I replied in English, with a few translations helpfully thrown in by people in the queue. It hardly moved because the matriarch was chatting with me, but nobody minded. The encounter ended with the lady getting her two daughters in the shop to stop work, change into the best clothes they had at hand, and pose with my family and me. She did not want copies of the photographs: They would not have Singapore in them. She wanted her daughters to look beautiful in *our* photographs: They are Italians. The queue lengthened in patience. On the way out, my teenage son got a hug and football stickers as presents.

I had merely seen the north; at the end of one day in the south, I had lived there for a lifetime. I sat on the balcony of my cheap hotel room, looking hundreds of metres down the cliff at the sea. I ate the pizza that I had bought from the shop down the road. It was the best that I had ever tasted. I opened the bottle of water purchased from the matriarch's shop. I felt like crying. How does one ever leave Sorrento?

Naples was different. Its gaunt and jagged grandeur was laced with danger in the air. Where were the Mafiosi? I looked around me. I was certain that they were there. They were merely not wearing dark glasses and carrying revolvers in their bulging pockets. An elderly gentleman was selling souvenirs. He approached me, not as they approach you in the successful north — purposefully, as if you are there because they are there — but hesitantly, almost apologetically: He was there because I was there. He was an aristocrat of poverty and decay, a chronicler of economies that had travelled to cheaper lands, taking lifestyles and customs with them. These aristocrats knew that their time had passed. I felt really bad for him and bought a black-and-white print of Naples — his vanished Naples. Where had it vanished?

I looked around for Walter Benjamin's Naples. He
speaks of almost a carnival where private and public
spaces merge into a single space of jostling selves. Just
as the living room, with its chairs, hearth, and altar, spills
onto the street, the loudness of the street "migrates into
the living room", he observes. "What distinguishes Naples
from other large cities is something it has in common with
the African kraal; each private attitude or act is permeated
by streams of communal life," Benjamin writes. "To exist,
for the Northern European the most private of affairs, is
here, as in the kraal, a collective matter."[1] Although I did
not see the astringent life of that collectivity — the only
migrations appeared to be those of tourists such as me who
had come to depart — the shopping mall was full of African
immigrants selling fake designer bags. A white boy came
over and yelled at them. They vanished in seconds. A police
car drew up, found nothing, and left. The Africans returned.
The kraal was happy.

I was not happy. The conducted tour went no farther
than Naples. Two more days, and we could have seen Sicily.
After all, the Bourbon Kingdom, the Two Sicilies, included
Naples and Sicily — Sicily, *The Leopard's* country.

The Leopard

"Between the pride and intellectuality of his mother and
the sensuality and irresponsibility of his father, poor Prince
Fabrizio lived in perpetual discontent under his Jove-like
frown, watching the ruin of his own class and his own
inheritance without ever making, still less wanting to make,
any move towards saving it."[2] Those striking lines appear

early in the book by Giuseppe Tomasi, the last prince of the great Sicilian family of Lampedusa. The liberal aristocrat died in 1957, unknown, impoverished, and childless, but leaving behind the manuscript of a novel that had been rejected for publication. *Il Gattopardo* (translated as *The Leopard* in English) — named after the family crest — is set in the era culminating in the creation of a united Italian kingdom in 1861. The Risorgimento, the movement for Italian unification, for which Giuseppe Garibaldi and his Redshirts campaigned, took off from Sicily. Prince Giulio Tomasi di Lampedusa, the writer's great-grandfather, represents elements of the feudal nobility that are most alert intellectually to their class's decline and fall, promised by the new dispensation. He takes the form of Don Fabrizio in the novel, which, in a metaphorical re-enactment of the theme of mortality running through the book, was published a year after the author's death. Reinforcing the theme of mortality, Edward Said, dying of cancer, reviewed it with his own approaching end in mind. His *Of Late Style* itself became a posthumous book.[3]

Immediately on publication, *The Leopard* established itself as a masterpiece of twentieth-century literature. As Lampedusa's fame spread across Europe, four sets of Italian critics attacked him. Devout Catholics found his pessimism excessive. Proud Sicilians were outraged by his portrayal of their society as a violent and irrational one. The literary Left did not find in the book the avant-garde and committed novel that it looked for. Devout Marxists were repelled by its seeming denial of the principle of progress in history.[4] Although, over on the French Left, Louis Aragon proclaimed it to be one of the great novels of all time, Elio Vittorini,

Alberto Moravia, and Franco Fortini accused it of being right wing.

I dare say that *The Leopard* is a right-wing masterpiece. Lampedusa's Prince, the novel's central figure, places inordinate and almost tendentious importance on non-human factors in Sicily's deterioration and descent into fatalism and violence. The landscape and the weather loom large in his denunciation. The Prince inveighs against "the atmosphere, the climate, the landscape of Sicily" as vindictive "forces which have formed our minds together with and perhaps more than alien pressure and varied invasions". Stalking its way through the book like a spell is "this landscape which knows no mean between sensuous sag and hellish drought; which is never petty, never ordinary, never relaxed, as should be a country made for rational beings to live in".[5] Again, Lampedusa blames the "violence of landscape, this cruelty of climate, this continual tension in everything" for the Sicilian character, "which is thus conditioned by events outside our control as well as by a terrifying insularity of mind".[6]

How predictable this is! Feudal leaders blame the landscape, the climate, and the times for the misfortunes of their subjects. There is history, too, to blame. Sicilians wince under the Prince's baronial gaze as he dismisses them with the imperious declaration that, "having been trampled on by a dozen different peoples, they think they have an imperial past which gives a right to a grand funeral".[7] With disarming honesty, Don Fabrizzo turns down an invitation to sit in the Senate, saying: "I am a member of the old ruling class, inevitably compromised with the Bourbon regime, and bound to it by chains of decency if not affection. I belong to an unlucky generation, swung between the old world and the new, and I find myself ill at ease in both."[8] The honesty is touching, but what about his despised Sicilian peasantry, swung between two worlds, between a past when it belonged to him, and a future that belongs to the opportunism of the new classes clever enough to profit from the revolution? The novel turns the pages on them in silence.

Similarly, we can empathize with the Leopard's loathing for the new rising classes which are trying to usurp the landed aristocracy's place in Sicilian history. They include parvenu merchants such as Russo, "with greedy eyes below a remorseless forehead", in whom Don Fabrizio finds "a perfect specimen of a class on its way up". Russo is "obsequious too, and even sincerely friendly in a way, for his cheating was done in the certainty of exercising a right".[9] There are others, too, on the make: the cynical young. Explaining why he does not wish to sit in the Senate, the Prince remarks caustically: "Now you need young men, bright young men, with minds asking 'how' rather than 'why', and who are good at masking, at blending I should say, their obvious personal interests with vague public ideals."[10] So we know what the rise of the bourgeoisie means for his class. But what does it mean for the peasantry? The Prince does not countenance that question, blaming instead Sicilians for repeating "what was written by Proudhon and some German Jew whose name I can't remember". The two men claimed that that the bad state of affairs "is all due to feudalism; that it's my fault, as it were". "Maybe," he exclaims peevishly, but argues that it cannot really be his fault because "there's been feudalism everywhere and foreign invasions too". The difference between Sicilians and others is, he taunts, the Sicilian ability to be dazzled by its own blindness. Here is the imperial trope at work again: It must be the sun that makes Sicilian eyes work this way!

The enervating effects of the Sicilian landscape and climate are a motif that borders on ecological determinism; the Prince's selective invocation of history is a neat effort to push responsibility elsewhere. A careful reader can hardly let him get away with that. Lampedusa's magisterial gestures collapse the great Southern Question — the political and cultural conflict over the Mezzogiorno — into a behavioural episode in Italian history. His Prince ignores a double irony about Sicily. The first irony is that it is a part of an Italy, which itself is seen as a southern European country because, following Italy's triumphal role in the Renaissance, Europe's centre of intellectual gravity moved to countries north of the Alps. The second irony is that, in the very act of unifying Italy, the 1860 Risorgimento accented the sense of north and south in the new nation.[11] Within that nation, the south brought with it a 400-year inheritance of exclusion that had followed the war of the Sicilian Vespers. "The Renaissance and the Reformation passed it by, leaving the islanders to the undiluted influence of Spain and the Counter-Reformation," David Gilmour writes. "Their intellectual and moral life declined and they lapsed into a neglected provincialism upon which even the Enlightenment made little impact."[12] Combine the two ironies, and it is not difficult to see why a double south emerged: a southern Italy that the north defined as an Other in Italy's quest for European modernity, and that it related liminally to Africa and the Orient; and a south whose economic and social distance from the north became a source of embarrassment within Italy.[13]

Even the masses of the industrial north, let alone their rulers, found it difficult to empathize with the poor of the agricultural south because they did not understand why the south was poor. The northern Italian saw the southerner in terms of the "organic incapacity of the inhabitants, their barbarity, their biological inferiority".[14] The truth, however, was that the south was poor, not because of some innate deficiency in its genetic or climatic stock, but because the Risorgimento had codified a system of regional disparities into a single state, where those disparities were exacerbated by the uneven development inherent in the spread of capitalism. Antonio Gramsci inserts into the Southern Question the memorable observation that "unity had not taken place on a basis of equality, but as hegemony of the North over the Mezzogiorno in a territorial version of the town-country relationship".[15] North and South engaged in a microcosmic class combat reminiscent of the struggle between town and country throughout history. Lampedusa exhibits no sympathy for the victims of this struggle.

Sicily's famed culture of violence reflects that divide — again, not some special culpability in the Sicilian character. In a perceptive study of social banditry, Hobsbawn locates the origins of the Mafia in the private and parallel system of power that grew beneath the oppressive, but inefficient rule of the Bourbon or Piedmontese state in Sicily. Throughout history, Sicilian peasants had lived under a double order: a foreign and largely remote central government, and a local dispensation of slave or feudal lords. Sicilian peasants had never regarded the central government as a real state, but "merely as a special form of brigand, whose soldiers, tax-gatherers, policemen and courts fell upon them from time to time". They had lived their lives between the lord's iron-fisted rule and his parasites, and their "own defensive customs and institutions". It was in this defensive space that the parallel system developed.[16] Its language was violence.

Here we come to the ideological heart of the novel. Fundamentally, the difference between Lampedusa and Gramsci is that for the liberal aristocrat, the Risorgimento destroyed too much; for the radical socialist, it destroyed too little. Gramsci's characterization of the Risorgimento as not really a revolutionary movement, but one of *transformismo* — the creation of a more extensive ruling class than before — is seen clearly in the choices made by the Prince's favourite nephew, Tancredi, who joins Garibaldi's fight, then breaks with the Redshirts to join the new Piedmontese army that attacks Garibaldi. In his sensitive reading of the novel — and the reworking of the novel in the film made by the red aristocrat Luchino Visconti — Said comments that Lampedusa is almost totally anti-Gramscian politically: Unlike Gramsci's call for pessimism of the intellect and optimism of the will in political work, the Prince exhibits a pessimism of both. *The Leopard* is "a southern answer to the Southern Question, without synthesis, transcendence, or hope".[17]

Politically, Lampedusa's Prince is the second figure of a secular trinity, the first being Niccolò Machiavelli's Prince and the third being Gramsci's Modern Prince. Machiavelli's Prince confronts Fortuna — the Classical Roman goddess of opportunity whom mediaeval Europe turned into a feared figure of capricous chance — with the robustly secular idea of *virtù*, the motivation and ability to succeed in Fortuna's world. Of course, Machiavelli recognizes that *virtù* cannot work if there is no opportunity, and that opportunity goes to waste if there is no *virtù*, but the emphasis in *The Prince* is thoroughly on possessing and using *virtù*. Its goal is to establish a unitary Italian state. It draws on the "literary concept of an Italy descended from Rome and destined to restore the order and the power of Rome", and it finds a workable model in the great absolute monarchies of France and Spain.[18] When Garibaldi's *virtù* fulfils Machiavelli's dream, Fortuna appears to Lampedusa's Prince and his class in the threatening form of a revolution that promises to lift the Sicilian masses into history. Surprised, annoyed, proud, and defiant of this challenge to his authority, the Leopard does not know how to respond. Refusing to fight for a cause that he knows is doomed, the Prince bows out of history. In due course Gramsci's Modern Prince, the hegemonic political party, will arrive. Machiavelli's Prince is an individual who seeks to represent the collective will out of the sheer exercise of personal will; he is a powerful, but ultimately a mythical creation. By contrast , the Modern Prince that Gramsci invokes is neither an individual nor is it mythical. It is the party, "a complex element of society in which a collective will, which has already been recognised and has to some extent asserted itself in action, begins to take concrete form".[19] The party sets out to give shape, meaning, and direction to a popular collective will by guiding it into history.

  In its portrayal of Don Fabrizio as he falls helplessly between the princely worlds of Machiavelli and Gramsci, the novel is anything but progressive. However, this fact does not diminish its aesthetic integrity because, as Lukács remarks, writers will tend to "present an inside picture of the class on which their own experience of society is based"; all other social classes "will tend to be seen from the outside".[20] Beyond this elementary reality, Lampedusa's sense of class indeed is informed by a redolent knowledge of the revolutions of 1848, the year in which Lewis Namier finds the "seed-plot of history" in his study of vanished supremacies.[21] Don Fabrizio knows his class too well to resist the inevitable. "We are not blind, my dear Father, we are just human beings... Holy Church has been granted an explicit promise of immortality; we, as a social class, have not," he says. "Any palliative which may give us another hundred years of life is like eternity to us. We may worry about our children and perhaps our grandchildren; but beyond what we can hope to stroke with these hands of ours we have no obligations."[22]

The Leopard's celebrated dictum — "If we want things to stay as they are, things will have to change"[23] — has passed into the lexicon of today's politics. Coming from anyone, it would become a maxim; coming from Lampedusa, it carries the emblematic credibility of history. "For the significance of a noble family lies entirely in its traditions, that is in its vital memories," the Prince says.[24] "We were the Leopards and Lions; those who'll take our place will be little jackals, hyenas".[25] What adds piquancy to this observation is, of course, the autobiographical element: The last Salina "is in effect the last Lampedusa, whose own cultivated melancholy, totally without self-pity, stands at the center of the novel, exiled from the continuing history of the twentieth century, enacting a state of anachronistic lateness with a compelling authenticity and an unyielding ascetic principle that rules out sentimentality and nostalgia".[26] So Said says.

What makes Lampedusa's Prince great, far, far greater than the feudal nobility is that, while accepting his fate as a member of his class, he can stand outside it, indeed, outside himself, and contemplate with brooding intensity, like a true philosopher, the impersonal course of mortality and change. The novel draws its magnetic power from the complexity of Don Fabrizio's character. He has "a certain energy with a tendency towards abstraction, a disposition to seek a shape for life from within himself and not in what he could wrest from others".[27] Herein lies the crux of the Prince's charm: He is a creation of a brutal system of wealth and power, but he plays his allotted role with an "elusive inwardness" marked by his "extraordinary self-sufficiency, his reserve, his fastidiousness and lack of greed, and above all his undiminished, if ultimately defeated, energy".[28] He is an individual who recognizes his place in the scheme of things. An avid astronomer, he is aware of "the sublime routine of the skies"[29] and is able to place own life in that overarching perspective.

The novel draws to an end with the Prince's death, whose import is magnified by the understatement with which it is portrayed. Bendicò, his beloved Great Dane, is also dead, but its carcass is embalmed as a symbol of the Prince's ties with his loyal place and time. Now comes the time to put the past in its place. The dog's body is thrown out of the window. "During the flight down from the window its form recomposed itself for an instant; in the air there seemed to be dancing a quadruped with long whiskers, its right foreleg raised in imprecation. Then all found peace in a little heap of livid dust."[30]

Some of *The Leopard*'s lines are sheer poetry. The poetry works by inviting those who do not share Lampedusa's view of history to extend a willing suspension of ideological disbelief to his characters, and to the Prince in particular.

His is a Homeric novel in the sense in which Auerbach refers to Homer's characters — who pursue us till we live with them, making the reality of their lives ours as well. Lampedusa's great achievement is to take us hostage forever in the Homeric manner in a book that is of such concision. Each sentence, each conversation, and each description is an exercise in economy, chiselled down to a sparse verbal perfection that etches itself on the mind forever. The incantatory lines of this very epigrammatic novel are easy to memorize because they are swathes of poetry interspersed with patches of prose.

Livid dust: that, finally, is the common fate of nobles, plebes, and palaces. In this world, meanwhile, we are all Sicilians — even those who turned back from history in Naples.

Notes

1. Walter Benjamin and Asja Lacis, "Naples", Benjamin, *Reflections*, op. cit., p. 171.
2. Giuseppe Tomasi di Lampedusa, *The Leopard*, translated from the Italian by Archibald Colquhoun (London: The Harvill Press, 1996), p. 7.
3. Edward W. Said, *On Late Style: Music and Literature Against the Grain* (New York: Vintage Books, 2007).
4. David Gilmour, *The Last Leopard: A Life of Giuseppe Tomasi di Lampedusa* (London: The Harvill Press, 2003), p. 186.
5. Lampedusa, *The Leopard*, op. cit., p. 123.
6. Ibid., p. 124.
7. Ibid., p. 127.
8. Ibid., pp. 124–25.
9. Ibid., p. 24.
10. Ibid., p. 125.

11. Nelson Moe, *The View from Vesuvius: Italian Culture and the Southern Question* (Berkeley, University of California Press, 2002).
12. Gilmour, *The Last Leopard*, op. cit., p. 176.
13. Moe, *The View from Vesuvius*, op. cit.
14. Antonio Gramsci, "Notes on Italian History", *Selections from the Prison Notebooks*, edited and translated by Quintin Hoare and Geoffrey Nowell Smith (London: Lawrence and Wishart, 1971), p. 71.
15. Ibid., pp. 70–71.
16. E.J. Hobsbawm, *Primitive Rebels: Studies in Archaic Forms of Social Movement in the 19ᵗʰ and 20ᵗʰ Centuries* (New York and London: W.W. Norton & Company, 1959), pp. 35–36.
17. Said, *On Late Style*, op. cit., p. 104.
18. Gramsci, "The Modern Prince", *Selections from the Prison Notebooks*, op. cit., p. 129.
19. Ibid.
20. Georg Lukács, *The Meaning of Contemporary Realism*, translated from the German by John and Necke Mander (London: Merlin Press, 1963), p. 94.
21. Lewis Namier, *Vanished Supremacies* (London: Hamish Hamilton, 1958).
22. Lampedusa, *The Leopard*, op. cit., p. 29.
23. Ibid., p. 21.
24. Ibid., p. 169.
25. Ibid., p. 128.
26. Said, *On Late Style*, op. cit., p. 107.
27. Lampedusa, *The Leopard*, op. cit., p. 94.
28. Said, *On Late Style*, op. cit., p. 109.
29. Lampedusa, *The Leopard*, op. cit., p. 30.
30. Ibid., p. 190.

7
England

Presidency College shares a playing field with Hare School, my father's school. Like the school, the establishment of the college in 1817 had opened an early chapter of the Bengal Renaissance. An extraordinary quickening of the senses accompanied every class or tutorial with our teachers at Presidency, most of whom had been students of the college themselves. They impressed on us the importance of not reading *backwards* into literature, of not imposing our values on the past in a regressive attempt to recover it for our age. Each age and its literature had to be judged on its own terms, which meant placing it in the tradition that it had grown from and the tradition that it had grown into. No age could be judged by extrapolating back into it what a subsequent age did, nor by looking in it for seeds of the future, except inasmuch as the earlier age had itself tilled the field. Thus, G.B. Harrison's scholarly approach to Shakespeare was dinned into us by the head of the department, the stern but saintly Professor Sailendra Kumar Sen. Harrison's approach rested on recreating Shakespeare's historical environment; recognizing the conditions of dramatic production in which he had functioned; and knowing the conditions of publication that had delivered to posterity his plays as printed texts.[1] To read Shakespeare meant viewing the Elizabethan world picture that he worked within, not least for its reflection in the Tudor view of history. This historical approach to literature was conservative; it was, to employ Sir Herbert Butterfield's analogous metaphor, a warning against a Whig interpretation of literature in which the written word from Chaucer to Browning is studied with reference to its receding distance from a centrally situated present. All the past then becomes a preparation for the present: Literature, like history, becomes a story of progress. We were permitted no such illusions, literary or historical.

Apart from the *dhuti*-clad Sailenbabu (*babu* is a term of respect), there were the Renaissance scholar Sukanta Chaudhuri — my tutor, who had received a Congratulatory First at Oxford — and Mrs Kajal Sengupta, who, too, had gone from Presidency to Oxford. There was also the Oxonian Arun Kumar Das Gupta. AKDG — we referred to our teachers by their initials — threw me, at least, into the deep end of the pool with a breezy instruction to read Basil Willey's *The Seventeenth Century Background*. I imagined that Willey's chapter on the rejection of scholasticism meant that, thenceforth, I could dispense with the scholarly approach to literature. Little did I suspect the torments of scholarship that awaited me! It was the first time in my life that I managed to read an entire book without understanding more than a tenth of it. It was AKDG's lectures on tragedy, where Albert Camus' *The Myth of Sisyphus* exchanged existential news with *King Lear*, which made me think that the examined life was, after all, worth living. *Dhuti*-clad Arunbabu, returning from his European exertions in college to his home in Beadon Street on time for his Hindu evening prayers, was a seamless and permanent rejection of all binary oppositions of East and West, Bengali and English. We ourselves, the students of the English Department, were all Bengalis and spoke Bengali among ourselves and to our teachers except in class and when we discussed our essays with them.

College over, I joined *The Statesman* as a subeditor in 1979. Although it was a conservative English-language newspaper that had begun life in colonial times, it had become an Indian institution even before the British had left in 1947. In 1943, it had published photographs that had made it impossible for the colonial authorities to deny the reality of the Bengal Famine. Then came India's independence. *The Statesman*'s pages now reflected how free India saw the world and how the world saw India. Again, it is extraordinary how a group of largely Bengali journalists chatted away in their tongue while producing India's premier English-language daily then. Under the distinguished editorship of S. Nihal Singh and Amalendu Das Gupta, who followed a long line of editors and who were succeeded by Sunanda K. Datta-Ray, *The Statesman*'s editorials were used by exacting fathers to teach their children how to write essays in the English language.

My eyes still longed for Cambridge though, where my father had arrived, courtesy of his quarrel with Professor Lasky. After five years with *The Statesman*, I left for *Asiaweek* in Hong Kong, where I was hired shortly to work for Singapore Press Holdings. I now made a living in the English language.

The road to Cambridge ran through Singapore. It was there that I met the person without whom there would have been no Cambridge for me. Charles Leslie Wayper was born in 1912. He studied at Newcastle Royal Grammar School and

St. Catharine's College, Cambridge, where he took a double first in the historical tripos. He was working on his doctoral thesis on Anglo-Austrian relations when World War II broke out and he was called up to join the Royal Army Ordnance Corps. However, a terrible accident, in which an American lorry rammed his motorcycle, threw him out of action for two years. After four operations, he was transferred to the Army Education Corps. Following the end of the War, he was appointed James Stuart Lecturer at the university, where he taught modern history and world affairs. For three decades from 1947, he was director of studies in history at Fitzwilliam House, during which time it became a full college of the university. He was President of Fitzwilliam College from 1970 to 1974, was appointed director of extramural studies for the university in 1977, and retired in 1980.[2]

I met Dr Wayper when he came to Singapore in 1986 to give a series of lectures to the staff of Singapore Press Holdings. I showed him my articles on foreign affairs. Since he liked some of them, I asked him whether he would agree to be one of my referees for my application to Cambridge. He agreed — Professor Arun Kumar Das Gupta was the other referee — and when I went up to Clare Hall in 1987, he agreed to supervise my Master of Philosophy thesis. He also supervised my Master of Letters thesis when I returned to Cambridge in 1992, thanks to the Raffles (Chevening) and S. Rajaratnam scholarships.

The first thing that strikes the new visitor to England is the truth of that old stereotype, its weather. English weather is nothing less than a religion; at least, its unpredictability is. It was left, therefore, to a heretical foreigner to reveal "the most striking thing about the English weather", which is that "there isn't very much of it".[3] However, the fact that the American heretic, Bill Bryson, is one of the chief converts to the English cause says much about the weather's mystique as well. The image of England created by George Orwell's "old maids biking to Holy Communion through the mists of the autumn mornings",[4] which has attained iconic status, derives its delicate astringency from a seamlessly understated union of weather, season, and faith. Far less poetic, of course, was the newspaper headline — "Heavy Channel Storms. Continent Isolated" — that has become a metaphor for provincial insularity. This is so not only because of the headline, but because English readers found nothing wrong with it!

Yet, if the English weather inspires and entitles its citizens to a divine sense of exceptionalism, there perhaps is a good reason for it: God is an Englishman. His country has not suffered a foreign invasion for 900 years; it has not had a revolution since the seventeenth century; and it has not had a civil war since the eighteenth century.[5] Since God is an Englishman, His English weather cannot but be a religion.

I was initiated into it when it began to snow, and I slipped on the sleet. Sitting on the road like a fool and looking around me helplessly as the English responded impeccably — by pretending not to notice the most obvious thing on earth — I said to myself: "Welcome to your father's Cambridge, Asad."

Englands

Perhaps no Bengali has gone farther than Nirad Chaudhuri in celebrating England. *A Passage to England* is a delightful account of what it is like for a lifelong lover of a country to find himself on its shores one day and to search in the flesh for what he sensed in the spirit long ago. Intellectually, as Chaudhuri says in *The Autobiography of an Unknown Indian*, his childhood knowledge of England was a chiaroscuro with "intense highlights in certain places and deep unrelieved shadows in others, so that what we knew gripped us with immeasurably greater power than it would have done had we seen it in more diffused and, consequently, more realistic light".[6]

Like Chaudhuri, I formed my idea of England from books. In a passage in *On England*, Earl Baldwin evokes an England of "the corncrake on a dewy morning"; "the sight of a plough team coming over the brow of a hill"; the "wild anemones in the woods in April"; and "the last load at night of hay being drawn down a lane as the twilight comes on, when you can scarcely distinguish the figures of the horses as they take it home to the farm". Above all, there is "the smell of wood smoke coming up in an autumn evening, or the smell of the scutch fires: that wood smoke that our ancestors, tens of thousands of years ago, must have caught on the air when they were coming home with the result of the day's forage, when they were still nomads, and when they were still roaming the forests and the plains of the continent of Europe".[7] This beautiful passage draws its authenticity from its author's lived and felt relationship with the countryside. Other writers pen Virgilian eclogues as they contemplate the quiet passage of generations through familiar terrain. This tangible attachment to the rural landscape, which becomes more moving as its nostalgic steps recede into elegiac longing, shapes the contours of the English imagination and is one of the most enduring features of the English identity.

Of course, any Arcadian idealization, of any landscape, obscures the problems of life today even as it reveals the lay of a lost land. With an earthy anger and reformative zeal worthy of Cobbett, Robertson Scott attacks the idea of attachment devoid of the need for change in his ironically named book, *England's Green & Pleasant Land*.[8] Naturally, the attachment grows less sentimental as the Industrial Revolution scars the rural landscape. Thus, J.B. Priestley speaks of three Englands. His first is the Old England of cathedrals, manor houses, inns, and parson, and squire. His second, industrial England, consists of railways, "sham Gothic churches", houses laid back-to-back, Unionist or Liberal Clubs, "a cynically devastated countryside, sooty dismal little towns, and still sootier grim fortress-like cities". His third, post-World War I England, belongs "far more to the age itself than to this particular island". With its bypass roads and its filling stations, its Woolworths and its motor coaches, and its "factory girls looking like actresses", its real birthplace is America.[9] D.H. Lawrence explores the English landscape in similar vein. Born to a miner near Nottingham in 1885, he speaks of a childhood spent in a "curious cross between industrialism and the old agricultural England of Shakespeare and Milton and Fielding and George Eliot".[10] What he finds intolerable are not the tribulations of a miner's life: they are present, but the miner's life is spent mostly underground, in an intimate male community where miners, working practically naked, develop an intuitive solidarity in the midst of the dangers facing them. What Lawrence cannot bear is the pervasive ugliness of the miners' daylight lives outside the fraternal pit. The "cold ugliness and raw materialism" of daylight life assault the collier's sense of beauty. "The real tragedy of England, as I see it, is the tragedy of ugliness," he exclaims. "The country is so lovely: the man-made England is so vile."[11]

Orwell picks up this theme of England underground. Like Lawrence, he finds the industrial landscape ugly, but unlike Lawrence, he does not romanticize the miners' underground life. Orwell observes coal miners at work and realizes with a shock, "what different universes people inhabit". Down in the invisible mine and its "lamp-lit world", wretched, subhuman work that is absolutely necessary for the life of the "daylight world above" goes on, but it is work that the world above is ignorant of and indifferent to. It is the anonymity of the coal miner's work that Orwell cannot bear, its misery kept safely out of the bourgeoisie's sight and the reach of contending ideologies that lay claim to the world. "For all the arts of peace coal is needed; if war breaks out it is needed all the more. In time of revolution the miner must go on working or the revolution must stop, for revolution as much as reaction needs coal," he says. "In order that Hitler may march the goose-step, that the Pope may denounce Bolshevism, that the cricket crowds may assemble at Lords, that the poets may scratch one another's backs, coal has got to be forthcoming."[12] Yet people in the sunlit world live on, oblivious to the human suffering inscribed into the lumps of coal whose faithful presence in their English lives they take for granted.

Orwell's appeal stems from his powers of close observation as an essayist, a talent that wins his polemical conceits a forgiving hand. After all, his maids biking their way to Holy Communion wend their way through a crowd of contradictory national characteristics: a hypocritical ignorance of the culpability of the Empire; an unteachable yet not altogether wicked ruling class; a general softening of manners brought on by capitalism; a general indisposition towards totalitarianism of either the Left or the Right; a sense of shame among intellectuals at their own nationality; and "the naked democracy of the swimming-pools".[13] No one treats these as serious sociological categories by which to judge Orwell's England fairly. Surely — perish the thought — his chaste maids do not pass by the naked democrats frolicking in the water. However, the sum total of his contradictory and even incompatible vignettes is an impressionistic portrait of English life that is broad enough to be probable, sceptical enough to be credible, and sharp enough to be indelible. Having repelled every idyllic intrusion into the English landscape, Orwell injects into it a tough realism and tangibility that gives it a further lease of emotive life.

Nirad Chaudhuri's frightful scholarship, spanning literature in Bengali, Sanskrit, English, Latin, and several other European languages, authenticates his allegiance to England as an idea. Unfortunately, that idea is also an imperial one; the virtues that he finds in English civilization stretch back irrevocably to imperial Greece. This obsession with empire must seem surprising in any grown man: The longing for someone else's empire truly is astonishing. The *Autobiography* is dedicated

To the memory of the British Empire in India,
Which conferred subjecthood upon us,

But withheld citizenship.
To which yet every one of us threw out the challenge:
'Civis Britannicus sum'
Because all that was good and living within us
Was made, shaped and quickened
By the same British rule.

In *Thy Hand, Great Anarch!*, the second part of his autobiography, Chaudhuri devotes a chapter to his faith in empires.[14] Reviewing the book, David Lelyveld exclaims: "Nirad Chaudhuri is a fiction created by the Indian writer of the same name — a bizarre, outrageous and magical transformation of that stock character of imperialist literature, the Bengali Babu."[15] Lelyveld continues: "Great cascades of flowery erudition, allusions to the histories of ancient Greece and endless quotations of French poetry are of interest mostly as evidence of Mr. Chaudhuri's artfully constructed persona."

Dr Wayper's Cambridge

Unlike Chaudhuri, I began my life in England by looking, not for the remnants of an empire, but for departures from it. I looked for Nora Handley and found her. I visited her once a week, and she told me the story of her life. The "black" man whose hand she had held had not been my father, but another Indian who had overtaken him in her affections. When that man graduated, he got ready to return to India. She wanted to marry him and leave with him, but he said that she would not be able to adapt to life in India. She said that she would follow him anywhere. He left without her;

she fell on the floor and cried. And she never married. As she recounted the event, she fell silent; I looked away.

When I returned to the university four years later, she was in a nursing home. My weekly pilgrimages continued, but her mind was wandering now. My father came to visit me in Singapore soon afterwards, and he was delighted that I had the telephone number of the nursing home. I called it, and she came to the phone. "Nora, this is Latif from Singapore," I said. "My father would like to speak to you." My father, who had called a professor a swine, said to me: "She is Miss Handley, not Nora." He took the phone. "Miss Handley, this is Latif from India. Do you remember me?" She said: "Of course I remember you. Why did you leave me crying on the floor?" My father was livid, but love selects its own memories. The very word "India" conjured up in her but one man and no other.

She died soon afterwards. I travelled to Britain a few years later. I found the tree, on the Cambridge Crematorium grounds, near to which her ashes had been interred. Lashed by the rain on a terrible evening, I placed flowers there, I, son of Latif from India, not of the Indian who had left her crying on the floor.

Meanwhile, I had worked with Dr Wayper. My M.Phil. thesis was on India's role in the birth of Bangladesh; my M.Litt. thesis was a comparative study of Singapore and Pakistan as new states. I was not unaware of the irony of my situation. I had studied English in Calcutta, and was now studying India and the rest of the subcontinent in Cambridge. But the irony had a logic. Presidency College was an indispensable part of the international landscape for the scholarly pursuit of English literature;

and Cambridge was indispensable equally for the study of the subcontinent.

The M.Phil. was in International Relations, a subject I had never studied. Along with Dr Wayper's supervision, lectures by Sir Harry Hinsley, Dr Richard Langhorne, Dr Ian Clark, Sir Elihu Lauterpacht, and Dr K. Subrahmanyam (who was the visiting Nehru Professor) helped me to grasp quickly the history and theory of international relations, strategic studies, and international law. Mercifully, we students did not have to grapple with the quantification of reality that awaited our compatriots in America, nor with the mystifications of theory that lurked in France. The Cambridge school was empirical. It was very much a part of the larger English tradition of international relations theory that derives its agency from having been mugged by history. My M. Litt., in History, was intermitted to three terms from six because I had the M.Phil.

Dr Wayper scrutinized my weekly essays closely. I was taken aback by the attention that he paid to grammar and structure. The proper place of a semicolon, the length of a paragraph, and the structure of the essay concerned him as much as my arguments did. His point was simple: If my meaning was not clear to myself, it could not be clear to others. I generally got off lightly. Dr Wayper was a man of great warmth, kindness and patience; the harshest rebuke that I earned from him was an aside that my point could stand if the moon were made of cheese. He was in a sardonic mood that day.

Cambridge was where I found Vinita Damodaran and Richard Grove, two historians whose intellectual companionship made me aware keenly of my shortcomings,

although their warmth never allowed me to feel bad about
this deficiency. A holiday which saw Richard driving the
three of us right up to the Scottish Highlands, with a running
commentary and occasional quarrels along the way, taught
me more about British history than I could have learned
from a dozen books. Poonam Mansingh, an M.Phil. student
in Social Anthropology from India who lived on college
premises as I did, provided another kind of warmth. Noticing
that I was well equipped for the English winter except for a
muffler, she advised me of the importance of not catching a
cold. Three days later, she had knitted me a green muffler,
woollen proof of the softest sisterly protection that I have
ever received from anyone.

During my second stint in Cambridge, I was not eligible
for college accommodation. I found a room in "Salix",
a house lying some distance from the city centre. My
landlady was Hanni Bretscher, widow of Egon Bretscher,
the Cambridge nuclear physicist who in 1944 had been a
member of the British mission to the Manhattan Project in
Los Alamos. A straight-talking, no-nonsense person, she
was kind. Having secured the rest of Salix, she would leave
the main door open at night so that a tramp could walk in
and sleep in one unlocked room of the house. On some
mornings, I would find that room slept in. Sadly, she died
in 1993, and Salix was sold.

On the social side of things, I joined the Cambridge
Union Society. Listening to debates is safer than taking
part in them. At one such debate, "This House would
like back, close its eyes, and think of England", I signed
up for the opposition. I had prepared what I thought was
a very witty speech. The audience thought otherwise. It

laughed, not with me, but at me. Then arrived a horrible moment when a speaker on the other side got the better of whatever little argument I had and was about to demolish it completely. I gave him a mournful look, as if to say: "First you colonised us. Then you drained our wealth. Now these churlish people are laughing at me. How can you do this to me?" He looked at me, changed tack, and spared me the *denouement*. Later, over drinks, I discovered that I had not done very badly. The laughter had been meant to throw me off track. I had not quite been thrown, for I had had no track at all.

Cambridge was not all fun: There was serious work, too. During my stay in Salix, I would cycle often to Shalimar, a good but reasonably priced Pakistani restaurant in the city centre. I would buy my dinner, and bring it back to eat later. One snowy night on a lonely road, I heard raucous laughter, and began to cycle faster. As I passed by the source of the drunken mirth — five female undergraduates — one said: "Get him." Since I was in no mood to be got and tried to cycle even faster, my amorous admirers felt scorned and went into a frenzy. One of them, sporting an arm like a piling column, hit me on the back with a thump that pushed my head almost into the wicker basket, which held my cherished *pulau* and chicken *tikka masala*. With a few more of such thumps, I could have eaten my dinner there and then. However, the thump had the beneficent effect of pushing the cycle away from the lascivious throng and giving me time to regain my balance. The thought of ending up as their dinner gave me such a fright that I cycled away from the lustful viragos at a speed that I had never reached before nor have achieved since.

Back at Salix, I told Farooq Swati, a fellow-boarder whose cycle I had borrowed, what had occurred. The tall and well-built man from Peshawar, whose piety and flowing beard would have made him a security threat these days, was a doctoral candidate in Archaeology. He is also the gentlest Muslim I have ever met. He sighed deeply and said that while a hot dinner was a good idea, getting beaten up by hot undergraduates was not. If the dinner came with the beating, perhaps I should stick to frozen food from Sainsbury's.

Cambridge was a dream. I kept in touch with Dr Wayper after I left university. Once, I stayed overnight at his cottage in Norfolk. He cooked dinner all by himself, redirecting my repeated offers of help to the neglected port. His wife had taught him to cook before she had died of cancer, he said, and he liked to cook occasionally. Later, when I stayed in his house in Cambridge, all that he permitted me to do was to make the tea and heat the dinner. As I left the next morning, he came to the door, which he had done on my weekly visits to him as a student. Every time, he would shut the door before I walked away. This time, he left it open and waited for me to get into the taxi. The door remained open as the taxi turned out of the driveway. I craned to see him. He was still standing there, at the open door, looking at me. The taxi took the road. I knew that I would never see him again. I never did.

When I received news of his death by email from his granddaughter, I stepped back from the computer. I knew so little about the man who had done so much for me. When he had spoken about himself, he had done so in an angular, third-person kind of way, as if life had found him while looking for everyone else as well. Even the motorcycle accident could have occurred to someone else, he had declared, with some other casualty having been thrown up by a world war involving millions. Wryly, he had put the accident, in which he had not been at fault, down to mysterious American driving habits. He had not been impersonal at all about others: He had been impersonal only about himself. Now he was gone. How does one respond to the death of someone so close and yet so private, distant and remote as to belong to an impersonal scheme of things?

When I visited Britain after my teacher's death, I travelled to the Cambridge Crematorium, where his ashes are interred next to his wife's by a tree in the garden, not far from Nora's. It was an awful evening, bitter, overcast, and windless. Although the tree was numbered, I could not find it in the vast garden. There was no one around. It was dark although dusk was still some time away. And then, just as I found the tree — and no one will believe me — the sun broke through the clouds, swathing the garden in pastoral hues, as the wind appeared from nowhere to lift the fallen leaves upwards and towards me. They clung to me. I walked to where he rested with his wife, and placed the flowers there.

Jathaba died in 1971, Nora — I mean Miss Handley — in 1995, my father in 2001, *Jethima* in 2003, and Dr Wayper in 2006. With their passage, my England is a quiet place now, somewhat aloof, mostly elegiac. But it remains my England.

Notes

1. G.B. Harrison, *Introducing Shakespeare* (Harmondsworth: Penguin Books, 1966, third edition), pp. 78–79.

2. Obituary, *The Times*, 28 April 2006, <http://www.timesonline. co.uk/tol/comment/obituaries/article710350.ece>.

3. Bill Bryson, *Notes from a Small Island* (London: Doubleday, 1995), p. 278.

4. George Orwell, "England Your England", *Inside the Whale and Other Essays* (Harmondsworth: Penguin Books, 1957), p. 64.

5. Donald Horne, *God is an Englishman* (Harmondsworth: Penguin Books, 1969), p. 13.

6 Nirad C. Chaudhuri, *The Autobiography of an Unknown Indian* (London: The Hogarth Press, 1987), p. 97. The book was first published in 1957.

7 Earl Baldwin, *On England* (Harmondsworth: Penguin Books, 1937), p. 16. The book was first published in 1926.

8. J.W. Robertson Scott, *England's Green & Pleasant Land* (Harmondsworth: Penguin Books, 1947). This is a revised and extended edition of the book that was first published in 1925.

9. J. B. Priestley, *English Journey* (Harmondsworth: Penguin, 1984), pp. 371–75. The work appeared originally in 1934.

10. D.H. Lawrence, *Selected Essays* (Harmondsworth: Penguin, 1950), p. 117.

11. Ibid., p. 119.

12. Orwell, "Down the Mine", *Inside the Whale and Other Essays*, op. cit., pp. 61–62.

13. Orwell, "England Your England", Ibid., p. 89.

14. Nirad C. Chaudhuri, *Thy Hand, Great Anarch!: India: 1921–1952* (London: The Hogarth Press, 1990), pp. 773–80. There was an earlier edition.

15. David Lelyveld, "The Notorious Unknown Indian", *New York Times*, 13 November 1988.

8
Champagne France

The programme for the trip to France in 2004 included an "optional" visit to the House of Moët & Chandon in the Champagne region. As the highway from Paris branched off into Epernay after two hours on the bus, rolling acres of vineyards and fairy-tale villages captured the view. The bus arrived at the company's headquarters, where the travellers from Asia were greeted by presence of a statue of Dom Perignon. Born Pierre Perignon in 1640, he entered the Benedictine Order at the Abbey of Saint-Vannes in Verdun at nineteen, and, when only twenty-eight, was appointed cellar master at the Abbey of Hautvillers. Stories that his blindness enhanced his tasting faculties are discounted today, as is the famous line that, on tasting the sparkling champagne that he had just invented, he declared: "Come quickly, I am drinking the stars!" Indeed, he did not invent champagne. But what this remarkable *viticulteur* possessed were special blending skills; apparently, he was also the first person to keep the sparkle in the wine by putting it in reinforced glass bottles and sealing it with Spanish corks. In the late 1920s, Moët & Chandon invoked his name for its *tête de cuvée*.[1] Although the champagne no longer owes its allure to being in very short supply always, the

Benedictine monk has become immortal in the enological imagination.

As my fellow-journalists and I alighted from the bus at Moët & Chandon's headquarters, we found standing, next to Dom Perignon's bronze statue, a fragile, feminine, and very French mortal. She was from the company's communication and heritage department and welcomed us with a mysterious smile to a tour of the premises. Her lispy tongue transformed the wine of English into the champagne of French. Thus, it would not do to say that wines were being fermented in underground cellars. "The grapes are sleeping in these caves," she whispered dreamily and looked at us. We agreed, and lowered our voices.

Champagne is, of course, not produced or made: It is created. So, too, was Moët & Chandon created and not established, according to a grand press kit we received that raised an historical toast to its mystique. In 1743, Claude Moët founded His House, which soon began supplying the royal and princely courts of France. The House of Moët became a favourite of the king's favourite, Madame de Pompadour, who proclaimed that champagne was "the only wine that leaves a woman beautiful after drinking". Monsieur Moët dutifully despatched 120 bottles to the Château de Compiègne every May, on time for the court's summer sojourn there. Later on, La Maison Moët also became the official supplier to the royal houses of England, Spain, Belgium, Sweden, and Denmark, as well as to the Vatican. The destiny of the House of Moët blossomed as the founder's grandson, Jean-Rémy, acquired vineyards abandoned since the Revolution of 1789 and improved facilities for pressing grapes, fermenting the juice, and bottling the wine. Jean-

Rémy Moët befriended the future Napoleon I, to whom the Brut Impérial would be dedicated, and Napoleon Bonaparte paid his first imperial visit to Epernay on 26 July 1807 on his return home after signing the Treaty of Tilsit. When the Franco-Prussian War of 1814 exposed the Epernay cellars to merciless Prussian and Cossack looting, Jean-Rémy declared prophetically: "All these officers who are ruining me now will make my fortune in the future. Those who are drinking my wine are also travellers who will spread the name of my House when they return to their countries." On 31 August 1816, Jean-Rémy's Moët's daughter married Pierre Gabriel Chandon de Briailles, creating Moët & Chandon.

The tour was over; we had not awakened the grapes. We made our way to the nineteenth-century Château de Saran, the family home located on the fringes of the Côte des Blancs, in one of the premier Chardonnay-growing districts of Champagne. There, the House entertains guests in the splendour of rooms that look out on serried rows of vines inhabiting a sleepily wooded hillside. We were received by our host, a man from the communication and heritage department whose regal bearing suggested that he, too, could have been founded in 1743 or thereabouts. We congregated on a vast terrace for the welcome drink. Lunch was served in a dining room situated off the drawing room, with a wooden screen enhancing the actual dining area's aura of privacy. At each place on the long and elegant table was the handwritten menu on thick vellum.[2] Mere mortals choose their wines according to the food they are destined to eat. At the Château de Saran, however, the opposite was true. The salmon and caviar, the main dish of pigeon, the cheeses, and the fruit platter had been chosen from all of earth's bounties because they were compatible with the Dom Perignon Vintage 1996 that started off the meal and the Nectar Impérial that concluded it.

The waiters served each course with a grandiose, extravagant, and carefully crafted series of gestures — which Roland Barthes would have called a meticulous "protocol of attentions"[3] — that turned lunch into an elaborate culinary ritual. The wine was raised to mythological heights that recalled Barthes' characterization of its role in French life as a "totem-drink, corresponding to the milk of the Dutch cow or the tea ceremonially taken by the British Royal Family". Knowing *"how* to drink is a national technique which serves to qualify the Frenchman".[4] Thus, someone's manner of holding the glass elicited an exclamation of scripted alarm from the shocked host; someone else's act of sipping the wine occasioned a philosophical discourse by him. Delighted by the performance of this Barthean spectacle, the guests egged him on, feigning ignorance and making mistakes wilfully to see how he would respond. He responded passionately although he knew that we were playing a game with him just as he was playing one with us. What was important was that we played our allotted roles: we as ignorant foreigners seeking initiation into the universal, yet inimitably distinctive, values of Gallic civilization; and he as the guide who possessed the power to grant or deny us entry to the realm of cultural salvation. True to Jean-Rémy's prophecy, the Asian hacks, like the Prussian and Cossack looters before them, spread the name of his House when they returned to their countries.

Notes

1. Andrew Jones, "Dom Perignon — Facts and Legends", *Wine on the Web*, <http://www.wineontheweb.com/dom_perignon/dom_perignon.html>.
2. Melissa Clark, "Maison Moet: Chateau de Saran", is a wonderful description of the hospitality offered at the château; <http://www.melissaclark.net/articles/archives/000032.html>.
3. Roland Barthes, *The Eiffel Tower and Other Mythologies*, op. cit., p. 143.
4. Roland Barthes, *Mythologies*, op. cit., pp. 59–60.

9
Two Bengali Greeks

And the reason is that human nature was
originally one and we were a whole, and
the desire and pursuit of the whole is called love.
— Plato, *Symposium*[1]

Rajkumar's and Rajkumari's paths crossed when they entered Presidency College, Calcutta, Rajkumari to read History, and Rajkumar, Bengali. Rajkumar did not restrict his exertions to the classroom; in fact, he did some reading lying where Rajkumari could study him between her classes. When the recluse stirred, he often made his way to the students' common room or the college canteen. His wiry frame did not stop him from once taking part in a hearty fight with a group of political rivals that left him with a bruised eye for a month. Graduating with a first-class Honours degree, he went on to read for his Masters in Bengali at Jadavpur University, also in Calcutta.[2]

Rajkumari had been rebellious from the time she could spell her name. She had grown up through a series of running street battles with the storm troopers of patriarchy — relatives, teachers, priests, and the like — who had dared to try and colonize the feminine imagination. After graduating from Presidency, she stayed on at Calcutta University to read for her Masters.

When I met Rajkumari in 2009, the fact that she and I were from Presidency College created an immediate bond between us, although we are separated by thirty years of age. I kept in touch with her through email and the occasional telephone call. Soon, I came to know of Rajkumar. They allowed me to wander into their lives, playing the friendly trespasser who was welcome to live vicariously through them if he so wished. I walked back to the college portico, the *agora* that each cohort vacates for the next only with the utmost difficulty. I had sat there three decades ago. Glancing back at the portico, I set up tent nostalgically in a far corner of their lives.

As Rajkumari surveyed the reclining Rajkumar, she saw a young man such as she had never seen before. He was handsome, interesting, suave, witty, combative, and he displayed a wry, cheeky insouciance guaranteed to draw the instant wrath of the powers that be. Most of all, he pretended not to need her. This pretence called for artfulness of the highest order, for Rajkumari was difficult to ignore. Set in a face that was radiantly fair, her eyes sparkled with a Dionysian abandon that set on fire the chiselled perfection of her Apollonian form. Ethereally thin, her features were so delicate that they threatened to dissolve in the first shower of monsoon. Yet, it was the elements themselves that announced her presence. Did the pretend stoic not notice, reclining in faked detachment, that a stormy restlessness was her *daemon*? She never walked, she never ran: Emerging from the wildest depths of riverine

Bengal, she flowed across ancestral time and waiting space, now to irrigate barren fields and then to drown grown men. She was talented, mercurial, tempestuous, irrepressible, determined, wilful, and beautiful. How could he be immune to her? Yet the sage kept his repose. When he did deign to rise and speak, he refused to recite poems to impress her or lose an argument to please her. What supreme nonchalance! Who did he think he was? A millionaire, an actor, a *swami*? He was none of these. He was more. He was her prince, for she was nothing if not a princess.

Thus did *eros*, the youngest student at Presidency, enter the story of the prince and the princess. Rajkumar and Rajkumari quarrelled in the morning, but were dancing in each other's eyes by noon. By evening, she was dancing on his head. Dusk meant parting for half an eternity. They travelled across Calcutta, learning its lovers' geography by heart but drawn to the river Hooghly, on whose banks they would sit and let their thoughts swim away and back together. Like Socrates himself, for whom there was never a day when he was not in love, Rajkumar and Rajkumari spent their days with each other, *eros*, and the world. Indeed, so close did Rajkumari and Rajkumar grow that jealous *eros* came and sat between them. Sometimes *eros* took the form of Rajkumar's *jhola* — the cloth bag in which the thinking Bengali keeps all his existential secrets and more — and at other times *eros* took the shape of Rajkumari's voluminously unruly files. But even though everlasting love kept a mischievous distance between the two young mortals, they found themselves transported to an erotic universe spanning fifth-century Athens and twenty-first-century Calcutta. They were Bengali Greeks.

The Erotic Polis

> *"For love, Socrates, is not, as you imagine, the love of the*
> *beautiful only." "What then?" "The love of generation and*
> *of birth in beauty."*
>
> — *Symposium*[3]

Diotima's glorious hymn in the *Symposium*, which even the wise Socrates needs to hear before he can move towards true comprehension of love, encapsulates the enduring power of *eros* — passionate, vehement love of the beautiful and, through it, of wisdom. Since the first time that Rajkumari observed the reclining Rajkumar, their lives have converged on the erotic principle, radiating a truth that a writer describes elegantly: "The beautiful, almost without any effort of our own, acquaints us with the mental event of conviction, and so pleasurable a mental state is this that ever afterwards one is willing to labor, struggle, wrestle with the world to locate enduring sources of conviction — to locate what is true."[4] Beauty "prepares us for justice".[5] And equality "is the heart of beauty" because equality is "the morally highest and best feature of the world".[6] When people confront beauty, it is not that they cease to occupy the centre of the world, for they had never done that in the first place: It is that they cease to stand even at the centre of their own world.[7]

Decentred by the erotic shock of each other's beauty, Rajkumari and Rajkumar have turned their gaze to the world that lies between them. The generation of which Diotima speaks can produce a virtuous deed, an educational discussion, a work of art, or a piece of legislation: For Rajkumar and Rajkumari, it is a desire to restore the health of a wounded *polis*. The contours of their *polis* emerge from the creation myth that Protagoras describes so movingly in the eponymous

Platonic dialogue. When the gods created mortal creatures, they charged Prometheus and Epimetheus with equipping each species with powers that would ensure its perpetuation. Epimetheus gave a species something special — strength, speed, or size — to ensure its preservation against other predatory species, or to prevent mutual slaughter. Having used up all his powers to protect beasts, he realized that he had forgotten man. Looking at helpless man, Prometheus stole from Hephaestus and Athena the gift of skill in the arts, and fire. This was good — and Prometheus duly paid his unforgettable price for having stolen fire from the gods — but it was not sufficient. Living in scattered groups, men were devoured by wild beasts, which they could not fight because they did not possess the art of politics, of which the art of war formed a part. So men founded fortified cities. These protected them from the beasts, but not from one another: Wanting political skill, they fought among themselves, and so scattered again to be at the mercy of the beasts. Zeus, fearing the total destruction of the human race, sent Hermes to impart to men the quality of respect for one another and a sense of justice for all, these being means to bring order to cities and create bonds of friendship. Unlike expertise in the arts, which was distributed unequally so that, for example, one trained doctor sufficed for many laymen, justice and respect were distributed to all alike because cities could not exist if only a few shared in those public virtues.[8] It was these common goods that protected men and women and gave them, in time, the freedom to seek generation and permanence in beauty.

Transformed by the power of each other's beauty, Rajkumar and Rajkumari seek to transform the world, to make its laws worthy of the beauty that both nature and the human mind exhibit. Held up in the mirror of each other's beauty, their sense of truth and justice has grown sharper and taken the form of a road. This is the road of politics which, for all its twists and turns, provides space for the realization of the highest goals in life. They take the lives of others personally. They refuse to believe that they should think only of their own births, or that their entry to Presidency College was nothing more than a personal achievement, or that the world is only about what they do or fail to do in life. They see their births as being among the millions of births that sustain life on a troubled but beautiful planet. They see their scholarly accomplishments not as hard-won trophies but as handmade weapons with which to defend those whom illiteracy and poverty condemn to timeless anonymity. Yes, they would have to make a living in the system — most likely as college teachers or university professors — but their lives would be larger than the system.

Even as they look back at the origins of the Protagorean city in the quest for security through justice, Rajkumari and Rajkumar look ahead to the *polis* as the guarantor of freedom through justice. Attempting to glimpse very heaven on soaring wings, they emerge into the awesome grand myth of the *Phaedrus*, where winged souls rise up to the rim of heaven to try and see the realm of truth that lies beyond it. To the gods, the vision is epiphanic, the sight sublime:

> When the souls we call 'immortal' reach the rim, they make their way to the outside and stand on the outer edge of heaven, and as they stand there the revolution carries them around,

while they gaze outward from the heaven... This region is
filled with true being... True being has no colour or form;
it is intangible, and visible only to intelligence, the soul's
guide. True being is the province of everything that counts
as true knowledge.

Feasting on the plain of truth, the mind of god observes
justice as it really is, which is self-control merged with
knowledge that is involved, not with change, but with things
as they really are. "This is how the gods live." As other
souls rise on their wings, their view is obstructed by their
baser longings and confusion. Many souls are "crippled"
and others have their wings severely damaged; all have to
leave without seeing things as they really are.[9]

Rajkumar and Rajkumari desire to arrive at justice
in their ideal *polis* through knowledge. However, being
decidedly agnostic if not almost atheist, neither of them
has much to do with Platonic reincarnations, with the
falling back to earth of mortals whose wings have been
damaged in the turbulent struggle to achieve the vision of
Forms by rising to heaven. They are not willing to wait ten
thousand years to be reincarnated and regain their wings.
Indeed, even the shortcut provided to the philosophical
lover — whose memory of Forms, roused by the sight of
beauty in the beloved, allows him to grow his wings again
in three thousand years — is too long for them.[10] Instead,
they draw strength from the Pindaric injunction: "O my
soul, do not aspire to immortal life, but exhaust the limits
of the possible". Like Dostoevsky's Kirilov, they believe in
immortality, not in the life hereafter, but in this life. *Eros*
has set the *polis* on fire in the here and now.[11]

Loving India

> *"It was a little like having to sweep away your footprints without a broom. Or worse, not being allowed to leave footprints at all."*
> — Arundhati Roy, *The God of Small Things*

In the *Symposium*, Plato makes an explicit connection between the passion of *eros* and the health of the *polis*. Indeed, the *Symposium* imagines the *polis* itself as the erotic society *par excellence*:

> Of what am I speaking? Of the sense of honour and dishonour, without which neither States nor individuals do any good or great work... And if there were only some way of contriving that a state or an army should be made up of lovers and their loves, they would be the very best governors of their own city, abstaining from all dishonour, and emulating one another in honour; and when fighting at each other's side, although a mere handful, they would overcome the world.[12]

In the *polis*, the "greatest and fairest sort of wisdom by far is that which is concerned with the ordering of states and families, and which is called temperance and justice".[13] *Eros* holds the key to this wisdom because "all men in all things serve him of their own free will, and where there is voluntary agreement, there, as the laws which are the lords of the city say, is justice".[14] To educate the young man in *eros* is to compel him "to contemplate and see the beauty of institutions and laws".[15] Admittedly, in the *Republic*, Plato harshly criticizes as an evil force the part of *eros* that is constituted by irrational desire; indeed, "the passion of sex has for so long been called a tyrant".[16] He traces the genesis of the tyrant in the licence and dissolution that become a master passion in the individual and overcome him like mania. "His passion tryannizes over him, a despot without restraint or law, and drives him (as a tyrant drives a state) into any venture that will profit itself and its gang, a gang collected partly from the evil company he keeps and partly from the impulses which these evil practices have freed within himself."[17] However, Plato's criticism is directed at the lustful aspect of *eros*, not at *eros* itself. Indeed, as he suggests in the *Symposium*, *eros* can be a weapon against despotism. Plato notes that, in a despotic system, "the interests of rulers require that their subjects should be poor in spirit; and that there should be no strong bond of friendship or society among them, which love, above all other motives, is likely to inspire, as our Athenian tyrants learned by experience".[18] Obviously, the truly erotic *polis* will not tolerate tyranny: it will strive to be a republic of desire serving the democracy of men and women.

Of course, in reality, the Athenian *polis* was a male preserve comprising only freeborn adult Athenian men: women, slaves, and foreigners were excluded. As with *eros* generally in the Socratic formulation, love for the *polis* was homoerotic.[19] That notwithstanding, in an essay on the citizen as lover, Susan Sara Monoson observes just how thickly and organically substantive the relationship between *eros* and *polis* was. In Pericles' funeral oration, Thucydides has him urge his fellow-citizens "to gaze, day after day, upon the power of the city and become her lovers *(erastai)*". Far from being just a turn of phrase, this metaphor suggests that democratic citizenship revolves around a notion of reciprocity between individual citizens and the *polis*. The metaphor "alludes to the highly formalized and valorized relations between adult, citizen men *(erastai)* and adolescent, freeborn boys *(erōmenoi)* that were common among Athenians. By appealing to citizens to conceive of themselves as 'lovers *(erastai)* of the polis,' Pericles is proposing that the Athenians can — *and should* — turn to their ordinary understanding of what it is like to love..."[20] Just how enthusiastically Pericles' call for total dedication to the *polis* was answered is "plain from the extraordinary record of Athenian activity in the years between 490 and 404 and the recognition on the part of Athens' enemies that they were facing no ordinary adversary". The Corinthians acknowledged that Athenians used their bodies "as if they were not their own and their minds as very much their own" in the service of their city.[21]

In his magnificent *Eros and Polis*, Paul Ludwig notes how *eros* provided classical thinkers with a bridge between the private and public spheres that is missing in modern thought. *Eros* was the most private of passions, but it went beyond love and sexuality to "embrace a wide variety of inclinations compromising ambition, patriotism, and other aspirations that were properly political in nature"; an example is the progression from being citizen-lovers to loving the city. Ludwig argues that the ancient conception of political *eros* helps underpin the "theoretical foundations of republicanism, including the foundations of modern representative and participatory democracies". Modern liberal democracy has lasted as long as it has because it permits the citizen to live a life of beauty and dignity created by the balance between personal liberty and civic dedication. However, since it is not easy to increase levels of liberty and dedication simultaneously, republican life will appear to fall short on both counts by turns. "Democratic citizens will therefore be vulnerable to longings that a liberal democracy cannot satisfy; longings both for greater individual autonomy and for stronger ties of obligation and affection among fellow citizens."[22] This dual desire for both autonomy and reciprocity, both privacy and affection, fires the political *eros* of Rajkumar and Rajkumari.

But there is more to their erotic consciousness. What gives Rajkumar's and Rajkumari's political *eros* its material edge is the state of the parliamentary Left in West Bengal, illuminated by a very post-ideological phenomenon: a left-wing ruling party using violence on poor peasants to "acquire" land for industry. Elenctic to the last, Rajkumar and Rajkumari do not believe in landless democracies. They refuse to love the land called India in the abstract; they love the land that belongs concretely to Indians. For Rajkumari and Rajkumar, to be in love is to love the state's unloved, for they are a part of the same erotic *polis*.

Looking Ahead

"What men or gods are these? What maidens loth?"
— Keats, *Ode on a Grecian Urn*

"Ithaca has given you the beautiful voyages.
And if you find her poor...
you must surely have understood by then what Ithacas
mean.
— Cavafy, *Ithaca*

"I am a part of all that I have met;"
— Tennyson, *Ulysses*

"[T]here's no reason why I shouldn't be charmed by you
every day, until you say I've had enough."
— Plato, *Charmides*

From a distant corner of their lives, I observe Rajkumari and
Rajkumar as they enter the Socratic life and the interplay
between its five fundamental forms of love. Charmed by
each other's footsteps, they have arrived in the realm of
eros. This they have done without abrogating the bonds of
storge, or familial love: The person Rajkumari loves most
after Rajkumar is her little brother. Then there is *xenia*,
love of strangers, including the wandering stranger whom
they invited into their lives and allowed to camp there.
There is *philia*, love of friends. Without the choric role
that friends play in Rajkumar's and Rajkumari's lives, half
their dramatic tension and energy would disappear; the two
reciprocate fully by participating in the lives and loves of
those friends. To look at this young crowd trudging through
laughter and tears together, with each friend a staff for the
others, is to be convinced of the claim made in the *Lysis*, that
"friendship exists only between good men" — and women
— "whereas the bad man never achieves true friendship with
either a good or a bad man".[23] Finally, there is *agape*, love
of humanity. I witnessed that quality in Rajkumari rather
unexpectedly. We had walked out of Presidency College
and crossed College Street on our way to the Coffee House,
when several street urchins accosted her. They obviously
knew her well because they surrounded her with raucous
familiarity, asking for money. As she searched in her purse
for coins in the melee, her cell phone dropped accidentally
from her hand. Rajkumari was aghast, but picked it up and
continued to fish for coins. Not a trace of anger crossed her

face. When I asked why she was so forgiving towards the children, she answered with searing simplicity: "Those who are certain of their next meal have time to agonise over more precious things. Children who have to beg to eat cannot be expected to care for others' belongings."[24]

In their ideal mix, these five forms of love advance true *aretẽ*: the pursuit of excellence that culminates in the quest for virtue. It is too soon to know how far Rajkumari and Rajkumar will move towards *aretẽ*. However, both of them are admirably clear about the direction that their lives are likely to take. Rajkumar is a prince without a principality. He promises Rajkumari not security and success, but peril and adventure. His politics has no easy destination, let alone a deadline. With Rajkumar, there is not the faintest chance of Rajkumari growing rich and fat. What he will do is preserve his own feral freedom because that is what drew Rajkumari to him in the first place. He will not respect her personal space, for he has none himself. She is his space. And here, although Rajkumari's ferocious streak of independence needs a continent-sized relationship to feel at home, she understands that when two people are close enough to be equal citizens of the erotic *polis*, it is their proximity that forms a common space large enough, not only for both, but also for a world in between. Rajkumar will never take ridiculous oaths such as promising to cherish her "like this forever", but, then, she will never ask him to do anything that silly. They know all too well the laws of determination — determination not in the sense of impersonal laws that deprive the individual will of its agency, but determination in the sense of boundaries of the possible within which individuals have to make their choices.

The laws of determination cause personal boundaries to expand or contract. Concrete choices are made within the contingent movements of those boundaries. Freedom lies in the recognition of that shifting necessity. So it will be with Rajkumar and Rajkumari. Citizens of the erotic *polis*, both will change, but in a world that they will still have to themselves. It will be a dangerous world, a painful world, and a difficult world, but also a world that will always be interesting and exciting and unpredictable, and new. It will be the eternal world of the ancient Greeks. This is how Rajkumari wants life to be. She wants to keep drawing closer to Rajkumar till, one day, infant India cradles softly in her arms.

Notes

1. *Dialogues of Plato*, The Jowett Translations, Justin D. Kaplan, ed. (New York: Washington Square Press, 1950), p. 192.
2. Rajkumar and Rajkumari — "prince" and "princess" in Bengali — are pseudonyms. The two protagonists wish to remain anonymous.
3. Ibid., p. 212.
4. Eliane Scarry, *On Beauty and Being Just* (Princeton and Oxford: Princeton University Press, 1999), p. 31.
5. Ibid., p. 78.
6. Ibid., p. 98.
7. Ibid., p. 112.
8. Plato, *Protagoras* and *Meno*, translated by W.K.C. Guthrie (Harmondsworth: Penguin, 1956), pp. 52–54.
9. Plato, *Phaedrus*, translated by Robin Waterfield (Oxford: Oxford University Press, 2002), pp. 30–31.
10. For a discussion of these aspects of the dialogue, see ibid., p. xxiii.

11. As for the two horses — one the very picture of self-control and the other of lust — that pull the chariot of the body in the *Phaedrus*, Rajkumari's and Rajkumar's ideas of transgression are modest by revolutionary standards. Rajkumari, a Hindu, has taken to eating forbidden food. She specializes in cheap beef; in order to stay trim, her other meals are frugal enough to keep saints pure. The patrician smokes cigarettes when she has the money; when she does not, she smokes plebeian *bidis*. However, in spite of her political radicalism, cooked in beef and laced with nicotine, she is deeply conservative in her morals. So is Rajkumar, another Hindu who is fighting the good war on his own diet of beef and nicotine.

12. *Dialogues of Plato*, op. cit., pp. 174–75.

13. Ibid., p. 215.

14. Ibid., p. 197.

15. Ibid., p. 217.

16. Plato, *The Republic*, translated by H.D.P. Lee (Harmondsworth: Penguin Books, 1955), p. 346.

17. Ibid., p. 348.

18. *Dialogues of Plato*, op. cit., p. 179.

19. The homoerotic nature of the Socratic *eros* does not pose a problem, however, in extrapolating its insights into the broadly heterosexual political culture of Calcutta and my two protagonists' quest for the erotic *polis*.

20. Susan Sara Monoson, *Plato's Democratic Entanglements: Athenian Politics and the Practice of Philosophy* (New Jersey: Princeton University Press, 2000), p. 64.

21. <http://europrogovision.blogspot.com/2008/01/erotic-patriotism. html>.

22. Paul W. Ludwig, *Eros and Polis: Desire and Community in Greek Political Theory* (Cambridge: Cambridge University Press, 2002), pp. 1–2.

23. Plato, *Lysis*, translated by Donald Watt, in Plato, *Early Socratic Dialogues*, Trevor J. Saunders, ed. (London: Penguin Books, 2005), p. 147.

24. For a fascinating study of these forms of love, see Christopher

Phillips, *Socrates in Love: Philosophy for a Die-Hard Romantic* (New York and London: W.W. Norton and Company, 2007). This book contemporizes Socrates' views on love, much as an earlier work does his philosophy in general: Christopher Phillips, *Socrates Cafe: A Fresh Taste of Philosophy* (New York and London: W.W. Norton and Company, 2001).

10
The Polish Hospital

Midway through a fifteen-day conducted tour of Eastern Europe in 2009, my wife, Mala, slipped in the snow in the Slovakian town of Banska Bysteria and fractured her left foot. The shock destroyed a kind of reverie that had enveloped me. Grand thoughts of visiting parts of the vanished Habsburg and Soviet empires had made me sign up for the trip although it was winter. Who could have blamed me? If, for roughly US$2,500, you were to fly from Singapore and see Munich, Salzburg, Vienna, Budapest, Banska Bysteria, Cracow, Auschwitz-Birkenau, Warsaw, Poznan, Berlin, Dresden, and Prague, you, too, would throw caution to the December winds and travel through the rolling plains, hilly roads, and sleepy villages that lie in one of the most historically charged parts of Europe. The tour of a lifetime turned out to be a nightmare sufficient for a lifetime, when, screaming in agony, my wife was carried aboard the tour coach. It made its way to Cracow, where the Hungarian driver, Kiseri Csaba, drove us straight to the 5th Military Clinical Hospital and Polyclinic. Sam Lee, the agreeable tour leader from Super Travels in Singapore, went about with his usual calm efficiency trying to get Mala admitted.

Since the tour bus was too large to enter the hospital premises without blocking other vehicles, the security guard ran inside and returned with a wheelchair. I pushed it into the Emergency ward, and Mala was admitted to hospital. Over the next four days, a string of doctors and nurses — particularly the English-speaking Doctors Michał de Lubicz Jaworowski, Dariusz Sienkiewicj, and Krzysztof Miśkowiec, and a nurse, Sister Natalia — cared for my wife as they would for a child too young to speak for, indeed, neither Mala nor I speak any Polish. One English-speaking doctor bought her a bottle of mineral water and taught her that the Polish word for the all-important painkillers was *nabol*; he also told the non-English-speaking nurses that she did not eat beef or pork. Another doctor found time to speak to her in his broken English even while attending to the two other patients in the room, elderly ladies who had suffered severe fractures. Neither of those ladies knew English, but one has a daughter who does, and the mother summoned her to the hospital so that she could speak to my wife and find out her needs. Grażyna Bożek turned up promptly. The relatives of other patients mistook Mala and me first for Albanians, and then for Mexicans. Now, because of Poland, we feel a special affinity for Albania and Mexico as well.

The insurance company in Singapore contacted the doctors in Cracow and, after having ascertained that my wife was fit enough to fly back home in her cast for her operation, arranged for an escort nurse from Prague to accompany her on Business Class. This arrangement agitated the Polish doctors greatly. Did Mala and I doubt their professionalism? No, she said: It was that she would have to remain under observation in hospital for ten days before the operation, that the insurance company was paying for her travel back home, that I was running out of cash, and that the Cracow hospital did not accept credit cards. The mention of money agitated the doctors even more. Dr Miśkowiec had said to me in the Emergency ward: "Even if you had no money, we would treat your wife because this is an emergency." Now, the doctors were wondering why I kept bringing up the question of money. They were interested in healing my wife's fractured foot. What was I interested in?

Unlike the hospital, Hotel Sympozjum is a business and is, therefore, interested in money. Yet, on hearing of my wife's accident, the staff's smiles gave way to concern. I could not pass by Reception without being stopped and asked about her progress. When I finally left the hotel, the porter carried my heavy luggage out to the taxi without expecting a tip. When he did receive the tip, he looked, not at the money that I had given him, but earnestly into my eyes as if to ask: "Are you sure?"

Meanwhile, the Singapore tour group had moved on. Mala and I had forced our son Abhilash to stick to the group because there was no point in his staying with us. For me, the trip from the hotel to the hospital and back was traumatic in temperatures that once dipped, I heard, to minus sixteen degrees Celsius. My body recoiled from the terror of a particularly nasty winter, and then my mind went blank. I wanted out of this accidental Habsburg/Soviet nightmare.

Yet, the nightmare opened my eyes to Polish realities that I would have passed by otherwise. Except for the kind of tourist who takes in the sights with a callousness that blinds him to people and events, a nation's quality of life is sensed, not from the state of the highway that runs from the airport to the city centre, but from the state of its public institutions, principally three: schools, hospitals, and prisons. I am too old for school, and I hope never to experience prison life first-hand, but my wife's misfortune enabled me to witness a slice of Polish life in hospital, and outside it.

I saw Mala and Lucie Radlova, her Czech escort nurse, off at Cracow airport. Over the next two days, I took a city tour of Cracow and visited Auschwitz-Birkenau before flying to Vienna to meet my son and the rest of the tour group for the flight back to Singapore. By then, Sister Lucie had checked Mala into the Singapore General Hospital.

Seeing Cracow

In the smoking area outside the Cracow airport building, I met an Afghan settled in Poland and working in Britain. Afghanistan was a war between East and West, he said. It was also a war between good and bad. Good Americans built schools for Afghan girls that bad Taleban burnt down. But bad Americans flew drones that killed Afghan children, something that incensed good Taleban. So who were good, the Taleban or the Americans, the Afghan children of the East or the American fighters of the West? He stubbed out his cigarette and left before I could ask him for the answer.

Similarly astringent was a conversation that I struck up with a woman who had grown up under communism. Yes, yes, there had been shortages of both goods and freedom under the old regime, she agreed. "But you don't spend your evenings talking about the freedom that you don't have," she said. "You look for things to do with the time that you have". What did Poles do? They attended Church, obviously. The communist state allowed spiritualism so long as people did not pray too loudly for its downfall. Poles could also attend classical concerts for a pittance, she said.

A common culture did for the mind what full employment did for the body: It gave people a stake in socialism because most people inhabited the same Polish world most of the time. The stake was real although the illegible ideology of the late-socialist Polish state inspired neither passion nor commitment. Now, the old problems were gone, but there was unemployment, people had become aggressive, and concert tickets were not cheap. I knew that. I knew also that there was homelessness, and that the harsh winter had been claiming homeless lives while Mala had slept in a warm hospital and I in a warm hotel room.

The woman's recollections of life under communism reminded me of Peter Brook. In his classic, *The Empty Space*, Brook pays the Polish theatre director Jerzy Grotowski a tribute by thanking Poland for him: "It is not by chance that the new metaphysical theatre of Grotowski arises in a country drenched in both Communism and Catholicism."[1] Jan Kott makes the point that the *Hamlet* produced in Cracow a few weeks after the 20th Congress of the Communist Party of the Soviet Union in 1956 was "modern and consistent, limited to one issue only": the political. It was political drama that drew its entire *raison d'etre* from the words "Something is rotten in the state of Denmark" and "Denmark's a prison".[2]

Every age, of course, has its own panoply of characters drawn from *Hamlet*, but Brecht, reading the play during World War II, wrote in his *Little Organum for the Theatre* that Hamlet's "reason is impractical when faced with irrational reality" and that he "falls a tragic victim to the discrepancy between his reasoning and his action".[3] Noting that Hamlet's "to be" means to avenge his father by assassinating the king, while "not to be" means giving up the fight,[4] Kott is gentler than is Brecht on the young man. Kott argues that Hamlet accepts the situation imposed on him, but revolts against it by refusing to let it define him beyond doubt. "He accepts the part, but is beyond and above it."[5] This is because he "considers life to be a lost cause from the outset" and "would rather be excused from this big game", but he "remains loyal to its rules".[6] Some people revolt against the world's cruelty, and others accept it as a law, but it crushes both.[7]

Poles produced by the Shakespearean era of Polish history still breathe the times. I tried to pick up a conversation with a middle-aged man waiting in the ward's corridor. "I do not speak English," he said testily in English. "*Ich kann kein Deutsch,*" he added for good measure. Was he making a point about the languages of the political transformation of Poland, where English and German are now the two favourite foreign languages? "Do you speak Russian?" I asked about the second language for Polish children in the old times. He threw me a long glance and walked away from a linguistic polity that no longer existed.

Other Women

The Cracow hospital, 5 Wojskowy Szpital Kliniczny z Polikliniką, shares its birth with the independence of Poland in 1918. Today, it is a military hospital only in name. Standing by my wife's bed in Room 13 of the Orthopaedics ward, it struck me that care for the human body is an aspect of the larger body politic. There was not in the Cracow hospital, as there is in many government hospitals in the Third World, a sense that the doctor belongs to a chosen race empowered to grant physical salvation to patients or to withhold it from them. (Singapore's hospitals, like the one in Cracow, are free of this stink emanating from the urinals of the feudal mind.) Instead, there was a modern democracy of companionship between doctors and patients united by a moody humanity that sometimes takes the form of health and, at other times, sickness. What mattered was the human body. It was sacrosanct, particularly because any injury to it — in the form of a fractured foot or a broken nose — tilted the balance between health and sickness intolerably in the latter's favour. That imbalance challenged society at large. It fell to doctors, manning the frontlines between health and sickness, to redress it. Medicine was a timeless battle of the spirit against the frailty of flesh.

Lying in a foreign hospital with a broken foot, my wife reminded me of the day that she had walked out of her parents' home for me and for an unknown world. Here, in this Polish hospital, we were not alone. The kindest of words came from a tongue unknown, people had time for her pain in the midst of their own, and, most of all, I was surrounded by the agency of medicine, the noblest pursuit known to universal man. Not just my wife but others in that room and ward, and other rooms and other wards, had taken refuge in that sanctuary. Bedridden, it is true, but this was Poland at its humane best.

That is why I was incensed during the city tour of Cracow. A certain advertisement for lingerie, which had stalked me from Budapest, if not Vienna, now suddenly insulted the very idea of the body that the hospital embodied and celebrated. Here, in public places such as bus stops, a woman placed her body in the service of no greater good than her very private lingerie. In doing so, the model's body became a commodity around which the lingerie draped itself. Normally, I do not worry too much about the exploitation of the adult female form in the media because it is a fact of adult life that I can do nothing about. But after I had spent time with my wife in hospital, where life can take on the sharpest of meanings, even facts of life about which I can do nothing became my business. The model was a work of God, created in Her own image. God's love had shaped the model's face and breasts, and hips and legs, to perfection — seamless and blameless — to be a source of pride and joy in being female and feminine. But here obviously was the post-1989 European woman, seen now in Budapest and then in Cracow and no doubt also in Warsaw and Prague, liberated from the totalitarian state only to be cast into the political economy of desire. Once, the state had tortured the body to induce conformity of spirit: Now, the market had bought off the spirit of a single, singular, authentic, and inviolable human being, to induce conformity of body.

What a mad world these wayward markets of desire create. Women would buy that brand of lingerie, especially if they could not afford it. Men would buy it, perhaps a pair for the dear wife, paid for by credit card, and another for the dear mistress (another day and in cash, of course). The gigolo would think of lingerie as a surprise for the gargoyle he served, but the danger was that she — what do you call her, master or mistress? — might actually fall in love with him in lingerie produced for models, not for not-so-baby elephants. The very thought convulsed him with laughter.

To lure people, intelligent gigolos aside, into buying that brand of lingerie, it was necessary that people own the model by consuming her. In some unspeakable act of sororal cannibalism, women passing by bus stops consumed her image so that it would make them as vulnerable and violable as a beautifully forlorn body commanding the lusts and loves of a million men. However, the market domesticated the model chiefly for men. Foolish men fantasized about bedding a model woman. All right, if the face was not that beautiful, the long legs would do, or the other way around. This model could be consumed in parts, like pieces of fried chicken: Breast or thigh or drumstick for you, sir? Traditional or spicy? Only very old men had no need for such choices: They would soon be providing standard meals for worms. Hence they cursed the model for mocking them with the eternal orgasm of imagined sex while worms made love underground. Poor model, she could not even laugh back at them, for she was frozen in advertising time.

All through history, women have been exploited in the name of biology or nature, or religion, or all of these. But only the market has succeeded in *freeing* woman to serve man through anonymous rituals of sexuality. The Church, so reliable a staff on the road out of totalitarianism, is now as helpless as the vanished communist party to stop this vandalism of the female form. Nobody is in charge of bus stops where a woman flaunts her body in post-communist glory. In the bad old times, a woman was not free to sell herself: In the good new times, she is. This is the real news being produced by the advertising factories of a very old sexual economy.

As the aircraft took off from Cracow, the bus stops were nowhere in sight, but a building seemed to stand, gauntly and kindly, on the far horizon of a city defined by a single word: *szpital*. When the hospital bill arrived in Singapore, I was amazed that Poland had charged me all of 816 PLN — about 200 euros — for having given my wife sanctuary during the nightmare of a lifetime.

Notes

1.   Peter Brook, *The Empty Space* (Harmondsworth: Penguin Books, 1972), p. 94.
2.   Jan Kott, *Shakespeare Our Contemporary*, op. cit., p. 48.
3.   Cited in ibid., p. 54.
4.   Ibid., p. 51.
5.   Ibid., p. 55.
6.   Ibid., p. 57.
7.   Ibid., p. 58.

11
Postmodern Europe

In a powerful critique of where the West stands today, John Gray avers that the Enlightenment project has ended, and has been replaced by a sense of value-pluralism that frees non-Western societies from being accountable to the Western *telos*. He diverges sharply from John Rawls's original position, a thought-experiment that eliminates from the legal order all references to individual conceptions of the good — and hence all potential for human division and conflict — so as to produce a society in which "no question can arise that does not have a solution acceptable to everyone".[1] Gray rejects the premise that such a solution is achievable and argues instead that the "post-modern condition of fractured perspectives and groundless practices" is an "historical fate".[2] Contrary to the Panglossian claims of the Enlightenment project — "the ruling project of the modern period" that was also "self-destroying" — the period has closed with "a renaissance of particularisms, ethnic and religious".[3]

The immediate source of Gray's deep discomfort is the downfall of the Soviet Union, which unleashed convulsions comparable to those attending the fall of the Roman Empire. The collapse of "the Enlightenment ideology of Marxism" did not result in a globalization of Western civil society, but led instead to "a recurrence to pre-communist traditions, with all their historic enmities, and in varieties of anarchy and tyranny".[4] His wider point is that the "humanist emancipatory project" of the Enlightenment has collapsed into nihilism, which is perhaps the only legacy that the Western movement will bequeath to a world where the West once had "humiliated" other forms of knowledge.[5] In the Counter-Enlightenment that is upon the West, its new missionaries — the nuns and novices training in the academic cathedrals of Western postmodernism — seek to translate nihilism into a universal condition.

Gray trains his anger on a fundamental Enlightenment approach to the world based on transforming knowledge, particularly scientific knowledge, into power over the environment, whose disastrous consequences are evident in the environmental degradation that the Soviet Enlightenment left behind, and which continues in the capitalist West. He worries about the ecological implications of this moment in history when, just as nihilism hollows out Western civilization at the very threshold of the West's economic universality, "non-Occidental cultures are asserting themselves against the West while accepting its legacy of a nihilist relationship with technology and the earth".[6]

Running through Gray's denunciation of the Enlightenment is a repudiation of the apotheosis of capitalism into neoliberalism. Capitalist rationality destroys, not only the macrocosmic environment that rises to become the protective benediction of the ozone layer, but the lived environment, consisting of attachments nurtured over generations that issue in local and national identities developed through loyalty to a common way of life. The invasions of nomadic capital attack, besiege, and pillage the habitus. Those attacked await universal economic salvation, but it never arrives for most of them. As Gray attends the Enlightenment's wake, he declares that enough is enough in this undeclared war. This is a powerful indictment, although it is not immediately clear what cultures, whether Occidental or Oriental, can do to get off capital's trajectory. Gray suggests abolishing the General Agreement on Tariffs and Trade (now the World Trade Organization), but how would that move, although grand in itself, protect national economies within, say, the European Union? Should the supranationalist project of the European Union be abandoned in favour of a return to national economies? But can even national economies protect citizens if Henri Lefebvre is right in defining the nation itself as nothing but the union of the market's geographical reach and the violence of the state?[7] Obviously, national economies cannot protect citizens unless it is possible to break the incestuous coerciveness inherent in the nation-state. That is an unlikely project. In an essay, "The Nation as an Imagined Economy", Satish Deshpande writes of Gandhi's radical opposition to a modern economy for independent India, of the kind that Nehru envisaged through a brand of socialist nationalism that installed "the figure of the patriot-producer as its chief deity".[8] Instead, Gandhi, in his ascetic piety, would ideally wish, Marx-like, to "abolish exchange value altogether, and live by the principle of use value", that is, "fulfilling one's personal needs through one's own labour".[9] That regression never occurred: It called for an implausible degree of economic sainthood.

Against Partiality

Like Gray, Amartya Sen is against the East's dialectical obsession with the West, which can take the two contradictory forms of admiration and dissatisfaction.[10] However, unlike Gray's, Sen's perspective does not depend on negating the legacy of the Enlightenment. For example, Gray thinks that liberal states must learn to live with illiberal states in peace and harmony.[11] The price of peace, he suggests, is that liberal states must be prepared to deal with non-liberal states on their own terms. But the question is whether illiberal states, too, will deal with liberal states on the latter's terms to pay for their share of the peace. Sen's argument is in many ways the opposite of Gray's. The colonized mind's fixation with the refracted life of the West has to be overcome, Sen declares, because it produces reactive self-identities. These colonial identities display a thorough dependency on the West even when they are opposed or hostile to it. "The dialectics of the captivated mind can lead to a deeply biased and parasitically reactive self-perception," he says.[12] The problem with the dialectics of dependence, he warns, is that colonized self-perception can exact a heavy price from the lives and freedoms of people by undermining their support for democracy and liberty in the non-Western world because these values are associated with a hated West. Unlike Gray, who would want the West to go its own way, Sen would not have the East go its own way if that means the repudiation of democracy and liberty. (In making this point, Sen does not imply, of course — and nor do I — that all Eastern societies are illiberal.) With an eye on terrorism, the most extreme form of a reactive self-identity, he notes how that identity can inflict vast damage on countries that are targeted for violent, retributive confrontation.[13] Partiality just will not do: The Orient has to be, *is*, much more than a creation of a departed colonialism.

Edward Said's rigorous struggle against partiality in the realm of letters gives *Orientalism* the passionate urgency of an intellectual manifesto. Dismayed by the easy and facile anti-Westernism spawned unintentionally by his immensely popular book, he found it necessary to restate, a quarter of a century later, the premises of his radical epistemology. "My idea in *Orientalism* is to use humanistic critique to open up the fields of struggle, to introduce a longer sequence of thought and analysis to replace the short bursts of polemical, thought-stopping fury that so imprison us," he wrote. His objective is to uphold the agency of humanism, or the ability to "use one's mind historically and rationally for the purposes of reflective understanding". By its very nature, humanism implies and is sustained by "a sense of community with other interpreters and other societies and periods". It is a collaborative project straddling East and West. In the humanist enterprise, "every domain is linked to every other one". These links and overlaps create, for discussions of issues of injustice and suffering, "a context that is amply situated in history, culture, and socio-economic reality". The public intellectual's role is to "widen the field of discussion".[14]

That is what Sen, one of today's leading public intellectuals, does in his difficult, but rewarding work, *Identity and Violence*. He advances an argument for hope based on a repudiation of a "solitarist" approach to human identity which seeks to partition people by placing them in singular and overarching categories. "Our shared humanity gets savagely challenged when the manifold divisions in the world are unified into one allegedly dominant system of classification — in terms of religion, or community, or culture, or nation, or civilization (treating each as uniquely powerful in the context of that particular approach to war and peace)," he writes.[15] Built on omissions and commissions that create a fictional singular identity, opposed fundamentally to other fictional singular identities, the illusion of destiny forms the ideational basis of violence because violence is ultimately the only way for implacably opposed identities to settle scores. The truth, however, is not only that a human being has many affiliations and identities, but that it is her right to decide how to prioritize her identities. Once a person is free to identify herself this way, she can interact with other, similarly free people in different ways.[16]

One way in which Europe can make it easier for the Orient to get over its past is by getting over its own sense of the past as a Grand Narrative. This is what David Gress does in his monumental work, *From Plato to NATO*,[17] where he dispenses with the narrative, that grand piece of Occidental self-imagery. As a narrative filled with "Magic Moments", such as Socrates drinking hemlock in defence of freedom, the West becomes a supposedly single trail of liberty and rationality running from Plato's *Republic* to Capitol Hill. America enters the Grand Narrative conveniently, and soon dominates it. Its nuclear might now guards the freedom trail, which runs from Capitol Hill to other capitals of capitalism *via* the North Atlantic Treaty Organization (NATO). In reality, no such trail exists from Athens, Greece, to Athens, Ohio, Gress suggests. Instead, he invokes two syntheses in the growth of the West from embryonic Europe: the synthesis of ancient, Christian, and Germanic cultures in late antiquity; and the synthesis of liberty, reason, and development in modernity. True, the second, modern synthesis emerged from the first and could not have occurred without it,[18] but they do not constitute a single story. By removing the Grand Narrative from the theatre of action, Gress clears the stage for a new engagement between the Occident and the Orient. True, the second synthesis — the colonial endeavour produced by the Enlightenment — still hangs over relations between the Europe and Asia, but with the Grand Narrative gone, the weight of European history on Asia is much less of a burden.

Indeed, the departure of the Grand Narrative reduces the need for Europeans to essentialize the West in defence of their place in the universal scheme of things. The West's values are not intrinsically Western, let alone exclusively Western. Sen warns importantly against a tendency in America and Europe to "extrapolate *backward* from the present" and claim that the primacy of freedom and democracy is a "fundamental and ancient" feature of Western thought and practice. Values emanating from the Enlightenment and "other relatively recent developments" cannot be considered to be a part of the millennia-long Western heritage. Rather, what classical authors such as Aristotle support are "selected *components* of the comprehensive notion" that constitutes the contemporary idea of political liberty. But writings in Asian traditions — Chinese, Indian, and Islamic — support such components as well.[19] Sen remarks pointedly that while the great Mughal Emperor Akbar, who reigned from 1556 to 1605, was trying to institutionalize religious tolerance in belief and practice, the Inquisitions were stampeding across Europe.[20] Simultaneously with their celebration of liberty, Western classics, like their Asian counterparts, do champion order and discipline, and so it is by no means clear to Sen that "Confucius is more authoritarian in this respect than, say, Plato or St. Augustine".[21]

I would add to Sen's comment E.H. Carr's astringent observation that no one has ever been able to live in Plato's republic.[22] Utopias of the good life, whether Asian or European, remain utopias; they take actual shape only when the unsuspected hand of contingency metamorphoses them into reality. It is historical contingency, and not utopia of one civilizational kind or another, that will decide whether Europe and Asia can work towards building a world that their young will want to inherit and inhabit. Europe has refreshed and replenished itself always through self-stabilization on a higher plane than the one that plunged it into crisis. "Man begins to detect in himself a new power by which he dares to challenge the power of time. He emerges from the mere flux of things, striving to eternize and immortalize human life," Ernst Cassirer writes. "In order to endure, the works of man must be constantly renewed and restored."[23] In order to endure, Europe must seek to stabilize itself on a plane higher than that at which it finds itself at the Enlightenment's wake. Only then can its sentiments, sensibilities, norms, values, and processes lay claim to universal agency.

The Ages of Europe

This could well happen if Europe shows the way to postmodernity. While the uncharitable aspects of postmodernity — particularly the fracturing of perspectives — are real enough, it has other characteristics as well. A primary characteristic is that the disappearance of jealous narratives and the decentring of certainties could reduce the need to kill for narratives. Postmodernism can contain the possibility of peace within and among nations. Here, Europe can lead the way.

Parag Khanna writes that it is no small thing Europe "invented, named, and shaped all eras of history".

> The classical world is defined by the flourishing of Greece; the Middle Ages followed the sacking of Rome; the European Renaissance led to the formation of nation states that organized the world in their image; and in the 21st century, Europe is pioneering the post-nation state regionalism and corresponding postmodern governance that is also being adopted around the world.[24]

True to its record of having invented historical eras, Europe is the first continent to move beyond the modernism that it created. Looking ahead to a world affected profoundly by the rise of postmodern Europe, Khanna believes that

> Other regions will similarly exhibit European-style hierarchies. China will have completed restoration of its ancient status as the "Middle Kingdom," presiding over half the world's population through its massive export volume, energy infrastructure feeding back to the core, and networks of Chinese diaspora. The world's third center of gravity will still be the United States, demographically stable but also more thoroughly blended with Latin America.[25]

How far Europe goes will depend, of course, on the outcome of the great drama of integration that is underway. Making a case against Euroscepticism, one perceptive author writes against treating as enemies Brussels' overworked bureaucrats, "most of them some kind of social democrats". The European Union might be boring, and even inefficient, but it is not malevolent.

> In its stiff and awkward friendliness it lacks even a hint of the late-Habsburg Kafkaesque. The European Union, seen from its insides in Brussels, has more in common with Habermas' philosophy. It is an extremely thorough and slowly grinding machine, it can be deadly boring, but it is honest in its own way and important to those whom it concerns.[26]

May I add that Europe concerns not only those who live in it, but those in the world beyond as well? If European supranationalism works, so might similar endeavours elsewhere, some day. If the European adventure collapses, a great failure would have been incurred.

Just how important postmodern Europe is, can clearly be seen from the British diplomat Robert Cooper's work on the European project.[27] He divides the world into three kinds of state. First are pre-modern states such as Somalia and Afghanistan where the state has failed and has unleashed a Hobbesian war of all against all. Second are the post-imperial, postmodern states of Europe, Canada, and perhaps Japan, which no longer think of security primarily in terms of conquest. Thirdly, there are modern states such as India, Pakistan, and China that follow traditional principles of *raison d'état*. The United States, too, would appear to belong in this category. Since regional organizations are a barometer of international postmodernity, Cooper draws attention to some of the institutions that underpin the

European postmodern state system. The most salient of
these institutions are, of course, the Treaty of Rome and the
Treaty on Conventional Forces in Europe, but there are also
the Organization for Security and Cooperation in Europe,
the Chemical Weapons Convention, the Ottawa Convention
that bans anti-personnel mines, the treaty that established
the International Criminal Court, the Strasbourg Court of
Human Rights, and the International Atomic Energy Agency,
among others.

Now, it is debatable whether even the European Union
is a genuinely postmodern organization. While it is true that
it has banished the national urge to resort to force *within*
Europe, it has not done so for theatres *outside* Europe.
Witness the participation of European countries in the
Afghan and Iraqi wars. The European Union's member
states have moved beyond the balance-of-power principle
among themselves, this principle being a key feature of
pre-modern and modern politics, but this move, although
radical in itself, is but a conservative attempt to secure a
better balance-of-power position for the European Union as
a whole *vis-à-vis* the United States, China, and other powers
down the line. All this said, however, the European goal of
achieving human security, security in its most comprehensive
sense, is incontrovertible. Whatever the future of Europe,
it is impossible not to glimpse aspects of its reality as a
postmodern project during even the most fleeting of visits
and the most cursory of encounters.

The Child in the Stroller

In May 2007, courtesy of the Asia-Europe Foundation
in Singapore, I found myself in Hamburg, taking part in

a seminar held on the sidelines of a gathering of foreign ministers of countries belonging to the Asia-Europe Meeting process. The seminar participants stayed in a hotel they shared with a large number of policemen and policewomen. They had been brought in to protect Hamburg from anti-globalization riots of the kind that had disrupted the Seattle meeting of the World Trade Organization in 1999, and that had caused one death in Genoa in 2001. It was surreal to meet the green-uniformed police for breakfast in the hotel's restaurant and exchange polite nods with them, only to encounter them or their colleagues later at the cordoned off Rathaus, the historic and ornate town hall of the Free and Hanseatic City of Hamburg that was the meeting's venue. What struck me was the youthfulness of the police, their relaxed bearing — their truncheons fixed to their belts looked more like fashion accessories than anything else — and their nonchalant helpfulness with road directions and so on. What struck me also was the presence of the police dogs, which snarled at passing innocents from their cages with a venom that I found almost ideological.

The protesters duly appeared and passed through Hamburg, although at some distance from the city hall. I found myself at the scene of action with a few of the other seminar participants. A marching column of humanity came down the street. Demonstrators chanted from trucks that carried wild banners fluttering to the beat of wilder music. Some demanded an end to the Iraq War. Some demanded an end to capitalism. More modestly, some demanded an end to debt repayment by the Third World. Rows of policemen stood with their truncheons and shields at the ready, or watched eagle-eyed from the riot control vehicles and water cannon trucks that blocked the marchers from entry into the restricted area.

As the procession went by, I witnessed an astonishing sight. A stroller with an infant and a triangular red flag was being wheeled by a man and a woman in deep discussion. As the tiny flag fluttered in the breeze, the child surveyed the icons of adulthood around him — the giant police vehicles and water cannon trucks — with the same equanimity that they observed him. This mini-anarchist was on a political outing with his parents. But who was responsible for him? Unless his parents were extremely irresponsible, it was obvious that they had complete faith in the habits of law practised by the very German state which they opposed.

Habits of law strong enough to keep the child of anarchists safe in the midst of anarchist violence: Now, that is what postmodern Europe is all about.

The Girl

At the Hamburg march, activists in T-shirts distributed pamphlets, sold booklets, and chatted up the crowd. A young woman was handing out pamphlets. She glanced at me, a class enemy wearing a suit, and hesitated to speak, before I said: "Hello." She was from a top German university. Radiant in her English — I wondered what her German would be like — she told me: "I am a Marxist."

> I asked her: "What do you study?"
> She said: "Law."
> I asked: "Do you intend to practise law?"
> She said: "Yes, if you mean how to break it."

> I asked: "What do you want to specialize in?"
> She said: "International law."
> I said: "Then I am sorry for you, because there isn't much of it left to break."

This piece of information elicited a giggle that rose from deep within her teenaged Marxist being. I said: "Look, there could be trouble-makers here. Take care." She laughed, as if to say: "Thanks, but I could be one of them." Her enigmatic laughter lingered in the Hamburg air long after she was gone. A human striving to break a law for states that exists almost in spite of them: how postmodern!

Lovers

My mind went back to my trip to Paris. Sitting in a park near the Invalides, I had seen two lovers at play. They had lain on the grass in a loose embrace. She suddenly sat on him, he pretended to be hurt and threw her off, she rolled on the grass, he reached out to her, and they broke out in shared laughter that wafted away into the rippling frolic of the breeze on the leaves. Two children played nearby, displaying the pre-sexual cunning with which little boys chase little girls. France was made for ease of love, growth, and procreation. And sharing. On a Montparnasse station platform where the train stood ready to leave for Chartres, I was having problems with the ticket-reading machine. A young couple was in a deep embrace nearby; he was seeing her off. She saw me from the corner of her right eye, disengaged herself with a kiss, helped me out, waved my thanks away, and returned to him in a seamless moment that had stolen nothing from their intimacy. As the train left, her eyes were moist for him.

Sex and News

The parents, the police, the giggling Marxist, and I were acting out our allotted roles on the European stage. We were participating in a spectacle. Let's face it: Postmodernism is about politics as spectacle. Spectacle plays an essential role in the governance of societies. In his 2001 Jefferson Lecture, Arthur Miller says that political leaders need to act in order to govern, by displaying the relaxed sincerity that constitutes the consummate actor's artistry,[28] because, as T.S. Eliot remarked, human beings cannot bear very much reality. Therefore, citizens take comfort vicariously from the fact that their leaders are bearing the burden of reality for them. Humans cloak their leaders with "a certain magical, extra-human, theatrical aura" to "help disguise one of the basic conditions of their employment — namely, a readiness to kill for us", [29] war being the ultimate sanction that reality can visit on a society. Combine this mystique, with which citizens vest and invoke their leaders/actors, with the mystifications of advertising and the subliminal influences of political spin that voters are subjected to, and it is easy to see how closely the political process is appropriated to a spectacle. Indeed, elections would not elicit enough interest to keep democracies functioning unless they were "assimilated to sporting events".[30]

However, the postmodern European still accepts democracy because its self-declared imperfection and capacity for self-correction show that the *demos* is humble and human enough to remain open to the possibility of incremental improvement through change. What frightens postmodern man is the teleological lure of religious perfection transferred to the political sphere, because he knows that the cunning of absolutism lies in tempting man with a promise that hides far more lethal contradictions and dangers than the ever-revealed contradictions of ever-imperfect democracy ever can. Eternity is the great enemy of democracy — indeed, of politics. Even in *The Leopard*, that most aristocratic of novels, Don Fabrizio's haughty disdain for young people who are enjoying themselves as the world of the Sicilian aristocracy falls apart, gives way to "compassion for all these ephemeral beings out to enjoy the tiny ray of light granted them between two shades, before the cradle, after the last spasms. How could one inveigh against those sure to die?" The Prince is willing to take them on their own fleeting terms because his philosophy is clear: "Nothing could be decently hated except eternity."[31] The time-bound judge themselves against eternity: The free are tired of it.

Since politics is spectacle and governance is a necessary way of acting, postmodern man himself is playful. Camus' definition of modern man — "he fornicated and read the papers" — loses some of its acerbic edge in postmodern times. Postmodern man plays at sex and reading. He thinks gamely. He embarks endearingly every morning on a vicarious odyssey through the world made print. He habitually mounts peaceful conquests at night (or whenever). He inhabits a world at play. And play is, of course, a very important activity: Johan Huizinga declares in *Homo Ludens* that the "great archetypal activities of human society are all permeated with play from the start".[32] Huizinga recalls Plato's intensely Saturnalian injunction in the *Laws* — that life "must be lived as play, playing certain games, making sacrifices, singing and dancing, and then a man will be able to propitiate the gods, and defend himself against his enemies, and win in the contest" — and commends it for exalting play to "the highest regions of the spirit".[33] Camus' reading and lovemaking are quintessential human festivities that require freedom: freedom from war, freedom from want, freedom to think, freedom to choose, and freedom to act.

On such insecure, even passing, but always defiant, freedoms hangs Europe's legacy to the world. As the magnificent choric ode in *Antigone* says, Zeus is "young through all time".[34] Zeus is young because time for him is an act of play. So might the playful European be at the end of twenty centuries.

Notes

1. Roger Scruton, *The West and the Rest*, op. cit., p. 10.
2. Gray, *Enlightenment's Wake*, op. cit., p. 219.
3. Ibid., p. 216.
4. Ibid., p. 217.
5. Ibid., pp. 219; 231.
6. Ibid., p. 269.
7. Henri Lefebvre, *The Production of Space*, translated by D. Nicholson-Smith (Oxford: Blackwell, 1991), p. 112.
8. Satish Despande, "The Nation as an Imagined Economy", *Contemporary India: A Sociological View* (New Delhi: Penguin Books, 2004), p. 63.
9. Ibid., p. 65.
10. Amartya Sen, *Identity and Violence: The Illusion of Destiny* (New York and London: W.W. Norton & Company, 2006), p. 85.

11. Gray, *Enlightenment's Wake*, op. cit., p. 233.
12. Sen, *Identity and Violence*, op. cit., p. 91.
13. Ibid., p. 93.
14. Edward Said, "*Orientalism* 25 Years Later: Worldly Humanism v. the Empire-builders", *Counterpunch*, 4 August 2003, <http://www.counterpunch.org/said08052003.html>.
15. Sen, *Identity and Violence*, op. cit., pp. xiii–xiv.
16. Ibid., p. xiv.
17. David Gress, *From Plato to NATO: The Idea of the West and Its Opponents* (New York: The Free Press, 1998).
18. Ibid., p. 48.
19. Amartya Sen, *Freedom as Development* (New York: Anchor Books, 2000), pp. 232–33.
20. Ibid., pp. 238–39.
21. Ibid., p. 234.
22. E. H. Carr, *The Twenty Years' Crisis 1919–1939: An Introduction to the Study of International Relations* (London: Macmillan, 1981), p. 8.
23. Ernst Cassirer, *An Essay on Man: An Introduction to A Philosophy of Human Culture* (New Haven and London: Yale University Press, 1944), p. 184.
24. Parag Khanna, "A Postmodern Middle Ages", op. cit.
25. Ibid.
26. Thomas Hylland Eriksen, "In Search of Brussels: Creolization, Insularity and Identity Dilemmas in Post-National Europe", J. Peter Burgess, ed., *Cultural Politics and Political Culture in Postmodern Europe*, Postmodern Studies 24 (Amsterdam and Atlanta: Rodopi, 1997), pp. 249–50.
27. Robert Cooper, *The Breaking of Nations: Order and Chaos in the Twenty-first Century* (New York: Grove Press, 2003); and Robert Cooper, "The New Liberal Imperialism", *The Observer*, 7 April 2002, <observer.guardian.co.uk/worldview/story/0,11581,680095,00.html>.
28. Arthur Miller, "American Playhouse: On Politics and the Art of Acting", *Harper's Magazine*, June 2001, p. 37.
29. Ibid., p. 43.

30. Northrop Frye, *The Modern Century* (Toronto: Oxford University Press, 1967), p. 28.
31. Giuseppe Tomasi di Lampedusa, *The Leopard*, op. cit., p. 154.
32. Johan Huizinga, *Homo Ludens: A Study of the Play Element in Culture* (London: Paladin, 1970), p. 22.
33. Ibid., pp. 37–38.
34. Sophocles, *The Three Theban Plays*, translated by Robert Fayles (New York: Penguin Books, 1984), p. 92.

Bibliography

Adorno, Theodor. *Minima Moralia: Reflections from Damaged Life*. Translated from the German by E.F.N. Jephcott. London: Verso, 1978.

Ambrosewicz-Jacobs, Jolanta, ed. *The Holocaust: Voices of Scholars*. Cracow: Centre for Holocaust Studies, Jagiellonian University, and the Auschwitz-Birkenau State Museum, 2009.

Arendt, Hannah. *Eichmann and the Holocaust*. London: Penguin Books, 2005.

Arnold, Matthew. *Culture and Anarchy and Other Writings*. Stefan Collini, ed. Cambridge: Cambridge University Press, 1993.

Auerbach, Erich. *Mimesis: The Representation of Reality in Western Literature*. Translated from the German by Willard R. Trask. New Jersey: Princeton University Press, 1968.

Badiou, Alain. "The Communist Hypothesis". *New Left Review* 49, January/February 2008.

Bakhtin, Mikhail. *Rabelais and His World*. Translated by Hélène Iswolsky. Bloomington: Indiana University Press, 1984.

Balakrishnan, Gopal. "Virgilian Visions". *New Left Review* 5, September/October 2000.

Earl Baldwin. *On England*. Harmondsworth: Penguin Books, 1937.

Barthes, Roland. *Mythologies*. Selected and translated from the French by Annette Lavers. London: Paladin Books, 1973.

———. *The Eiffel Tower and Other Mythologies*. Translated by Richard Howard. Berkeley: University of California Press, 1977.

Baudrillard, Jean. "The Pyres of Autumn". *New Left Review* 37, January/February 2006.

Benjamin, Walter. *Illuminations*. Translated by Harry Zohn. New York: Schocken Books, 2007.

———. *Reflections*. Translated by Edmund Jephcott. New York: Schocken Books, 1986.

Berlin, Isaiah. *The Crooked Timber of Humanity*. Henry Hardy, ed. Princeton: Princeton University Press, 1998.

Berman, Marshall. *Adventures in Marxism*. London and New York: Verso, 1999.

Bernasconi, Robert. *Sartre*. London: Granta Books, 2006.

Bonet, Joana. "Starbucks Democracy". *La Vanguardia*, 10 June 2009.

Brook, Peter. *The Empty Space*. Harmondsworth: Penguin Books, 1972.

Bryson, Bill. *Notes from a Small Island*. London: Doubleday, 1995.

Buruma, Ian and Avishai Margalit. *Occidentalism: The West in the Eyes of its Enemies*. New York: Penguin, 2005.

Camus, Albert. *The Fall*. Translated by Justin O'Brien. Harmondsworth: Penguin Books, 1957.

Carr, E.H. *The Twenty Years' Crisis 1919–1939: An Introduction to the Study of International Relations*. London: Macmillan, 1981.

Cassirer, Ernst. *An Essay on Man: An Introduction to A Philosophy of Human Culture*. New Haven and London: Yale University Press, 1944.

Cavafy, Constantine P. *The Complete Poems of Cavafy*. Translated by Rae Dalven. San Diego, New York and London: Harvest, 1976.

Chaudhuri, Nirad C. *The Autobiography of an Unknown Indian*. London: The Hogarth Press, 1987.

———. *Thy Hand, Great Anarch!: India: 1921–1952*. London: The Hogarth Press, 1990.

Cooper, Robert. "The New Liberal Imperialism". *The Observer*, 7 April 2002.

———. *The Breaking of Nations: Order and Chaos in the Twenty-first Century*. New York: Grove Press, 2003.

Despande, Satish. *Contemporary India: A Sociological View*. New Delhi: Penguin Books, 2004.

Eco, Umberto. "Tolerance and the Intolerable". *Index on Censorship*. May/June 1994.

Eriksen, Thomas Hylland. "In Search of Brussels: Creolization, Insularity and Identity Dilemmas in Post-National Europe". In *Cultural Politics and Political Culture in Postmodern Europe*, edited by

J. Peter Burgess. Postmodern Studies 24. Amsterdam and Atlanta: Rodopi, 1997.

Finley, M.I. *Aspects of Antiquity: Discoveries and Controversies*. New York and London, Penguin Books, second edition, 1977.

Frye, Northrop. *The Modern Century*. Toronto: Oxford University Press, 1967.

Garton Ash, Timothy. "1989 Changed the World. But Where Now for Europe?". *The Guardian*, 4 November 2009.

———. "1989!" *New York Review of Books* 56, no. 17 (5 November 2009).

———. "A More Civil World". *Index on Censorship*, 23, no. 6 (November/December 1994).

Geertz, Clifford. *Islam Observed: Religious Development in Morocco and Indonesia*. Chicago and London: The University of Chicago Press, 1971.

Gilmour, David. *The Last Leopard: A Life of Giuseppe Tomasi di Lampedusa*. London: The Harvill Press, 2003.

Gramsci, Antonio. *Selections from the Prison Notebooks*. Edited and translated by Quintin Hoare and Geoffrey Nowell Smith. London: Lawrence and Wishart, 1971.

Grass, Günter. *On Writing and Politics 1967–1983*. Translated by Ralph Manheim. San Diego, New York and London: Harcourt, 1985.

Gray, John. *Enlightenment's Wake*. London and New York: Routledge Classics, 2007.

Gress, David. *From Plato to NATO: The Idea of the West and Its Opponents*. New York: The Free Press, 1998.

Hampson, Norman. *The Enlightenment*. Harmondsworth: Penguin Books, 1968.

Harrison, G.B. *Introducing Shakespeare*. Harmondsworth: Penguin Books, third edition, 1966.

Heikkilä, Tuomas, ed. *Europe 2050: Challenges of the Future, Heritage of the Past*. Helsinki: Edita, 2006.

———. "The Middle Ages and the Birth of Europe". In *Europe 2050: Challenges of the Future, Heritage of the Past*, edited by Tuomas Heikkilä. Helsinki: Edita, 2006.

Hobsbawm, E.J. *Primitive Rebels: Studies in Archaic Forms of Social Movement in the 19th and 20th Centuries.* New York and London: W.W. Norton & Company, 1959.

———. *The Age of Capital: 1948–1875.* New York: Vintage Books, 1996.

Horne, Donald. *God is an Englishman.* Harmondsworth: Penguin Books, 1969.

Huizinga, Johan. *Homo Ludens: A Study of the Play Element in Culture.* London: Paladin, 1970.

Keen, Maurice. "Mediaeval Ideas of History". In *The Mediaeval World.* General editors David Daiches and Anthony Thorlby. London: Aldus Books, 1973.

Khanna, Parag. "A Postmodern Middle Ages". *Spiegel* Online, 23 July 2009.

Klima, Ivan. "Freedom and Garbage". *Index on Censorship* 23, no. 6 (November/December 1994).

Konwicki, Tadeusz. *A Minor Apocalypse.* Translated from the Polish by Richard Lourie. New York: Vintage Books, 1984.

Kott, Jan. *Shakespeare Our Contemporary.* Translated by Boleslaw Taborski. London: Routledge, second, revised edition 1967.

Kundera, Milan. "The Tragedy of Central Europe". Translated by Edmund White. *New York Review of Books*, 26 April 1984. Reprinted in Gale Stokes, ed. *From Stalinism to Pluralism: A Documentary History of Eastern Europe Since 1945.* New York and Oxford: Oxford University Press, 1991.

———. *The Unbearable Lightness of Being.* Translated from the Czech by Michael Henry Heim. London: Faber and Faber, 1999.

di Lampedusa, Giuseppe Tomasi. *The Leopard.* Translated from the Italian by Archibald Colquhoun. London: The Harvill Press, 1996.

Lawrence, D.H. *Selected Essays.* Harmondsworth: Penguin, 1950.

Lefebvre, Henri. *The Production of Space.* Translated by D. Nicholson-Smith. Oxford: Blackwell, 1991.

Lelyveld, David. "The Notorious Unknown Indian". *New York Times*, 13 November 1988.

Levey, Michael. *Early Renaissance.* Harmondsworth: Penguin, 1967.

Lévi-Strauss, Claude. *Tristes Tropiques.* Translated from the French by John and Doreen Weightman. New York: Penguin Books, 1992.

Liddle, Rod. "It's Not just the Swiss — all Europe Is Ready to Revolt". *The Spectator*, 2 December 2009.

Ludwig, Paul W. *Eros and Polis: Desire and Community in Greek Political Theory.* Cambridge: Cambridge University Press, 2002.

Lukács, Georg. *The Meaning of Contemporary Realism.* Translated from the German by John and Necke Mander. London: Merlin Press, 1963.

de Madariaga, Salvador. *Portrait of Europe.* New York: Roy Publishers, 1955.

Maier, Charles S. "Holocaust Fatigue". In *The Holocaust: Voices of Scholars*, edited by Jolanta Ambrosewicz-Jacobs. Cracow: Centre for Holocaust Studies, Jagiellonian University, and the Auschwitz-Birkenau State Museum, 2009.

Miller, Arthur. "American Playhouse: On Politics and the Art of Acting". *Harper's Magazine*, June 2001.

Moe, Nelson. *The View from Vesuvius: Italian Culture and the Southern Question.* Berkeley, University of California Press, 2002.

Monosan, Susan Sara. *Plato's Democratic Entanglements: Athenian Politics and the Practice of Philosophy.* New Jersey: Princeton University Press, 2000.

Namier, Lewis. *Vanished Supremacies.* London: Hamish Hamilton, 1958.

Nietzsche, Friedrich. *The Birth of Tragedy and The Genealogy of Morals.* Translated by Francis Golffing. New York: Doubleday Anchor Books, 1956.

Ortega y Gasset, José. *The Revolt of the Masses.* Anonymous translator. New York and London: W.W. Norton, 1957.

Orwell, George. *Inside the Whale and Other Essays.* Harmondsworth: Penguin Books, 1957.

Pagden, Anthony Pagden, ed. *The Idea of Europe: From Antiquity to the European Union.* Cambridge: Cambridge University Press, 2002.

Panofsky, Erwin. "Artist, Scientist, Genius: Notes on the 'Renaissance-Dammerung'". *The Renaissance: Six Essays*. New York: Harper Torchbooks, 1962.

Parsons, Craig. *A Certain Idea of Europe*. Ithaca: Cornell University Press, 2006.

Phillips, Christopher. *Socrates Cafe: A Fresh Taste of Philosophy*. New York and London: W.W. Norton and Company, 2001.

———. *Socrates in Love: Philosophy for a Die-Hard Romantic*. New York and London: W.W. Norton and Company, 2007.

Pieterse, Jan Nederveen and Bhikhu Parekh, eds. *The Decolonization of Imagination: Culture, Knowledge and Power*. London and New Jersey: Zed Books, 1995.

———. "Shifting Imaginaries: Decolonization, Internal Decolonization, Postcoloniality". In *The Decolonization of Imagination: Culture, Knowledge and Power*, edited by Jan Nederveen Pieterse and Bhikhu Parekh. London and New Jersey: Zed Books, 1995.

Plato. *Dialogues of Plato*. Edition featuring the Jowett Translations, edited by Justin D. Kaplan. New York: Washington Square Press, 1950.

———. *Lysis*. Translated by Donald Watt. In Plato, *Early Socratic Dialogues*, edited by Trevor J. Saunders. London: Penguin Books, 2005.

———. *Phaedrus*. Translated by Robin Waterfield. Oxford: Oxford University Press, 2002.

———. *Protagoras* and *Meno*. Translated by W.K.C. Guthrie. Harmondsworth: Penguin, 1956.

———. *The Republic*. Translated by H.D.P. Lee. Harmondsworth: Penguin Books, 1955.

Pomorska, Krystyna. "Foreword". In Mikhail Bakhtin, *Rabelais and His World*. Translated by Hélène Iswolsky. Bloomington: Indiana University Press, 1984.

Prawer, S.S. *Karl Marx and World Literature*. Oxford: Oxford University Press, 1978.

Priestley, J.B. *English Journey*. Harmondsworth: Penguin, 1984.

Quattrocchi, Angelo and Tom Nairn. *The Beginning of the End: France, May 1968*. London and New York: Verso, 1998.

Riemen, Rob. *Nobility of Spirit: A Forgotten Ideal*. Foreword by George Steiner. New Haven: Yale University Press, 2009.

Robertson Scott, J.W. *England's Green & Pleasant Land*. Harmondsworth: Penguin Books, 1947.

Romano, Sergio. *An Outline of European History from 1789 to 1989*. Translated from the Italian with the assistance of Lynn Gunzberg. Oxford and New York: Berghahn Books, 1999.

Rubinstein, Richard E. *Aristotle's Children: How Christians, Muslims, and Jews Rediscovered Ancient Wisdom and Illuminated the Middle Ages*. Orlando: Harvest Books, 2004.

Said, Edward W. *On Late Style: Music and Literature Against the Grain*. New York: Vintage Books, 2007.

———. *Orientalism: Western Conceptions of the Orient*. Harmondsworth: Penguin, 1985.

———. *"Orientalism* 25 Years Later: Worldly Humanism v. the Empire-builders"*. Counterpunch*, 4 August 2003.

Scarry, Elaine. *On Beauty and Being Just*. Princeton and Oxford: Princeton University Press, 1999.

Schlögel, Karl. "Archipelago Europe". *eurozine*.

Scruton, Roger. *The West and the Rest: Globalization and the Terrorist Threat*. London and New York: Continuum, 2002.

Sen, Amartya. *Freedom as Development*. New York: Anchor Books, 2000.

———. *Identity and Violence: The Illusion of Destiny*. New York and London: W.W. Norton & Company, 2006.

Singer, Isaac Bashevis. *In My Father's Court: A Memoir*. Harmondsworth: Penguin Books, 1979.

Sophocles. *The Three Theban Plays*. Translated by Robert Fayles. New York: Penguin Books, 1984.

Steiner, George. *The Idea of Europe*. Amsterdam: Nexus Institute, 2005.

———. *Language and Silence: Essays 1958–1966*. Harmondsworth: Penguin Books, 1969.

Stokes, Gale, ed. *From Stalinism to Pluralism: A Documentary History of Eastern Europe Since 1945*. New York and Oxford: Oxford University Press, 1991.

Tagore, Rabindranath. *Nationalism*. Introduction by Ramachandra Guha. New Delhi: Penguin Books India, 2009.

de Unamuno, Miguel. *The Tragic Sense of Life in Men and Nations*. Translated by Anthony Kerrigan. New Jersey: Princeton University Press, 1972.

Väyrynen, Raimo. "Old and New Borders in Europe". In *Europe 2050: Challenges of the Future, Heritage of the Past*, edited by Tuomas Heikkilä. Helsinki: Edita, 2006.

Wallerstein, Immanuel. *The Capitalist World Economy*. Cambridge University Press, Cambridge 1979.

———. *The Modern World System II: Mercantilism and the Consolidation of the European World-Economy, 1600–1750*. New York: Academic Press, 1980.

———. *The Modern World System III: The Second Era of Great Expansion of the Capitalist World-Economy, 1730–1840s*. San Diego: Academic Press, 1989.

———. *The Modern World System: Capitalist Agriculture and the Origins of the European World Economy in the Sixteenth Century*. New York and London: Academic Press, 1997.

Webber, Jonathan. "Auschwitz: Whose History, Whose Memory?". In *The Holocaust: Voices of Scholars*, edited by Jolanta Ambrosewicz-Jacobs. Cracow: Centre for Holocaust Studies, Jagiellonian University, and the Auschwitz-Birkenau State Museum, 2009.

Index

ABOUT THE AUTHOR

Asad-ul Iqbal Latif is a Visiting Research Fellow at the Institute of Southeast Asian Studies (ISEAS), Singapore. His areas of research include Singapore's political and strategic relations with China, India, and the United States. He is the author of *Hearts of Resilience: Singapore's Community Engagement Programme* (2011), *Wang Gungwu — Junzi Scholar-Gentleman: In Conversation with Asad-ul Iqbal Latif* (2010), *Lim Kim San: A Builder of Singapore* (2009), *Three Sides in Search of a Triangle: Singapore-America-India Relations* (2009), *India in the Making of Singapore* (2008), and *Between Rising Powers: China, Singapore and India* (2007). He co-edited (with Yeo Lay Hwee) *Asia and Europe: Essays and Speeches by Tommy Koh* (2000).

Asad graduated with Honours in English from Presidency College, Calcutta, and received his Master of Letters degree in History at Clare Hall, Cambridge, where he was Raffles (Chevening) and S. Rajaratnam Scholar. He was a member of the president's committee of the Cambridge Union Society, and a member of the editorial committee of the *Cambridge Review of International Affairs*.

Asad was a Fulbright Visiting Scholar at Harvard University's Weatherhead Center for International Affairs. A journalist before joining ISEAS, he worked at *The Statesman* in Calcutta, *Asiaweek* in Hong Kong, and *The Business Times* and *The Straits Times* in Singapore. He was a Jefferson Fellow at the East-West Center in Hawaii.

www.ingramcontent.com/pod-product-compliance
Lightning Source LLC
Chambersburg PA
CBHW020000290326
41935CB00007B/251